FOREX TRADING

The Ultimate and Complete Beginner's
Guide with Three Simple Strategies, Tools, Money
Management and Psychology for Long and Short-Term
Investment Opportunities in the Forex Market

LARRY JONES

To my family,
for their love, patience and support

Disclaimer

Please note that everything in this book has been written for educational purposes only and does not serve as an official lesson or training in trading Forex. You will not be qualified or certified as a professional trader in any way, shape, or form through reading this book. Instead, you will discover information regarding what has worked, at times, for other traders in the past and what has supported other traders in experiencing positive returns on their investments.

The author is not registered as a securities broker-dealer or investment adviser and is not licensed to provide investment advice. This book should only be used as an educational tool and is not a replacement for professional investment advice.

Furthermore, past results do not guarantee future profits, meaning that this book makes no claims to guarantee you, or anyone else, profits through trading Forex. You recognize that by reading this book and choosing to participate in the Forex market, you are solely responsible and liable for your results. The author and anyone else involved in the making, publishing, and distributing of this book are in no way liable for any results you may experience when trading Forex.

Forex trading involves high risk and may lead to losses. Losses can and will occur. No system or methodology that has ever been developed can guarantee profits or ensure freedom from losses. Any losses made or any unfortunate turn of events due to investments made by the readers of this book will be at the investor's risk. This means that you understand that any losses, no matter how catastrophic, are solely your own responsibility. The author of this content is not in any way liable for personal trade decisions and will not provide compensation to any individual who may lose money trading Forex or any other financial instruments.

By reading this document, the reader agrees that under no circumstances, the author or the publisher is responsible for any financial loss, injury, or damage, direct or indirect, to persons or property arising from the use of the information contained in this book.

Contents

Introduction

Congratulations on buying your copy of *Forex Trading*. You have made the right choice in purchasing this book out of the many options available. Forex Trading is a book that seeks to enlighten your mind and open your eyes to the secrets that lead to success in trading the Forex market. Probably, you are currently struggling to make a profit and have already encountered many losses, or you are just starting in Forex trading. In both cases, this book is for you.

Forex Trading is a book that has been outlined in a simple way. It uses easy everyday language, with illustrations and graphical examples that make the understanding easier even for rookie traders.

This book is focused on four fundamental aspects that play a role in Forex trading. First, I introduce you to Forex trading and provide an overview of the Forex market. I help you understand what Forex trading is in the simplest language ever. Secondly, I introduce you to the analysis of the market and some analytical tools. This will help you understand how to find the best opportunities and when to invest. The best tools are vital to any person who wishes to find success in the market. You will learn about some of the available options and how to utilize these tools properly. Thirdly, the book focuses on three simple strategies, explaining them step-by-step. Very often, after finishing a trading book, you may feel lost, and you don't know where to start in practice. With this book, I will take you by the hand and bring you to your first trade in the Forex market. Lastly, the book focuses on how to write your trading plan and how to avoid some common mistakes. There are only two factors that determine success in Forex trading. One is developing the right mindset to avoid mistakes, and the second one is using data and analytical tools correctly.

Forex trading is a lucrative investment opportunity that can help you transform your living standards in a very short time. However, for you to gain considerable success in this field, you must be willing to learn. Those who succeed in Forex trading take time to analyze the markets and study trends. They are eager to burn the midnight oil, learn analytical tools, and invest a lot of time in data mining to ensure that they make the right decision. This book is your first step in becoming a successful Forex trader.

Without further ado, hop on and enjoy the ride as we venture deep into the secret world of Wall Street millionaires.

Happy reading!

1 The Basics of Forex Trading

Before we move into the mathematical and technical terms of the subject, we need to have a basic understanding of Forex. In this chapter, we will look at some of the basic terms that every Forex trader must understand. Forex trading has its language. If you want to be a master at trading, you must first grasp the basics. You must know the definition of basic terms such as crosses, pips, spread, etc. Once you understand what these terms mean and how they are relevant to your trade, we will move deeper into the application and the processes that lead to success in Forex trading.

Forex Market Overview

Forex, or foreign exchange trading, refers to a network of buyers and sellers who transfer currencies between each other through the facilitation of banking institutions and trading agents. The transactions are done under an agreed market price, mainly determined by trade activity and other factors such as political and social events. Forex is the only option available for individuals, institutions, and banks to convert one currency to another. If you have traveled across borders, you have probably been required to exchange your currency and perhaps have tried a Forex trade. In most cases, people use Forex to change their money for practical use. However, in Forex trading, the main aim is to make an income.

The amount of currency exchanged each day can determine the price of the same currency. In other words, just like any other commodity, currencies are subject to the forces of supply and demand. If a specific currency is in high demand, the chances are that its prices will rise. The fluctuations in the amount of currency traded make the value of currencies very volatile. It is such volatility that makes Forex trading an attractive business. If you are a trader, you can easily capitalize on moments of fluctuation to gain a profit. With that in mind, you must also realize that the market's volatility introduces a huge risk. As much as you can turn a trade into a lot of money in just a few seconds, you can equally lose a considerable amount of money. This business is like the battle of kingdoms. You can't stay in the middle ground. You must either win or lose, and losing means going out of business.

If you are thinking about trading in Forex, you must have already considered stock markets. Stock trading and Forex trading are similar but have their differences. In stock trading, buyers and sellers mainly exchange publicly traded shares or commodities in regulated markets (like the New York Stock Exchange). Unlike the stock market, Forex trading does not take place on exchange markets, but it is done on a peer-to-peer basis in OTC (Over-The-Counter) markets. Forex trading happens across the world, run by a network of banks with four major centers in different time zones. The major trading zones include London, New York, Sydney, and Tokyo. However, even with the trading centers located in different time zones, there is no time limitation to trading Forex. You can trade at any time of the day.

There are three main types of Forex markets:

- **Spot Forex market:** This mainly refers to the direct exchange of physical currency. It usually takes place at the exact point of exchange, hence the name spot exchange. This type of exchange can be done, for example, at a bank branch or at the airport when you are traveling to a new territory.

- **Forward Forex market:** This trade involves signing an agreement that sets a date for purchasing a certain currency at a specified price. This type of trade involves a considerable risk but is also more profitable if the trade turns out well. When you trade a Forward Forex transaction, you agree upon the price and exchange date in the future. This type of trade is mainly used for speculation purposes and provides room for profit among commercial traders.

- **Future Forex market:** This is similar to forwarding trading, only that it is more formal and binding. Forward trading can just be a signed agreement between two individuals and is not recognized by most legal institutions. On the other hand, future trading is a practice that is well recognized by most financial institutions and governments. A binding agreement of future trade must be fulfilled by the parties involved. Traders who make future trades are usually basing their purchases on speculation. They do not plan on taking the currency itself but aim at making a profit from the trade. Depending on your understanding of the market and your analytical ability, you may either make a profit from making a future sale or a future purchase.

Forex vs. Stock Trading

In this book, you are going to focus on Forex trading, although you could choose to trade stocks too. In Spot Forex trading, there are plenty of currencies traded, so you have many options like in the stock market. However, most traders only deal with some major pairs (in particular, EUR/USD, GBP/USD, JPY/USD, and USD/CHF). This is one of the reasons why Forex is a better option. Trading Forex is much simpler since it is easier to keep an eye on a limited number of options. Instead, in the NYSE alone, there are over 2800 listed stocks. Keeping an eye on most of these stocks requires some serious dedication and hard work. On the other hand, a Forex trader may choose to focus on the few most-traded currency pairs. Furthermore, it is also possible to invest in Forex with small accounts (a few thousands of dollars), without any kind of limitation, and with the possibility to manage the risk properly.

Here are some factors to consider when deciding between Forex and stock markets.

Trading Hours: The Forex market is the most promising in this area, allowing you to trade around the clock. Forex markets are open twenty-four hours a day, from Sunday 4:00 P.M. to Friday 4:00 P.M. EST. On the contrary, stock markets are traded based on your time zone and within the stipulated trading hours. For instance, the NYSE stock exchange market is open Monday to Friday from 9:30 A.M. to 4:00 P.M. EST. Such limitations make it impossible for you to maximize your profits. You may realize that most Forex traders start serious analysis and trading after working hours. On the other hand, stock traders must pay full attention to the trade during trading hours and use any moment available at their disposal to manage the trades. Further, Forex traders enjoy the possibility to trade in the US, Asian, and European market hours no matter the location.

Terms of commission: When considering trades, you must think about profit margins. The profit you earn is, to a large extent, influenced by the trading platforms and broker commissions. In stock markets, it is compulsory to surrender a commission that may be as high as 10% of your profit. Thankfully, Forex trading does not present such challenges. Only a few Forex brokers require a commission to such high levels. If you consider the tight and consistent spread, Forex trading becomes a much better option than stock trading. In Forex trading, brokers are usually compensated for their services through the bid-ask spread. We will delve much deeper into the details of broker compensation and spread as we continue.

High Liquidity: Given that Forex trading can be done anywhere at any time, it is much more flexible than stock trading. There is high liquidity in the Forex market, which means that transactions are executed on the spot. In most cases, the transactions are executed at the prices shown at the time of the transaction. This is a significant advantage over many stocks that lack liquidity. You may enter a trade expecting to gain a certain profit, but you get a price worse than you expected because of the delay in the time of entry or exit or because of the lack of liquidity. This can seriously affect the result of your trade and your income. If you are looking for a trade option where you can instantly execute your transactions and make money according to your market predictions without being influenced by other forces, Forex should be your choice.

With that said, the execution of orders under Forex trading

depends on the trading conditions. Most brokers only guarantee stop, limit, and entry orders under a regular market.
If external forces have influenced the market, the situation
changes, and you may have to wait a little longer to execute
your orders. This should not be a cause for alarm, considering
that it is not the normality, and it happens not so often.

Intermediaries Involvement: Stock trading happens over a
centralized market. There are plenty of advantages in a centralized market, such as access to all trades and information,
but there is the disadvantage of middlemen. Stock traders
have to work their way through intermediaries before they can
make a profit. Any party in between you and the security you
are trading is a liability. Thankfully, you can engage in spot
currency trading without the need to have other people dictate
your choices. Forex traders have the advantage of dealing with
the market directly, and as a result, they get better deals at a
cheaper cost.

Analysts and Large Funds Influence: In the stock market,
large fund buying is a common occurrence. Large traders can
sell stocks among themselves and end up determining prices.
On the contrary, in Forex trading, the market is too large and
too complex to be influenced by a single trader. Spot Forex
trading involves governments, central banks, hedge funds, retail currency converters, and large net worth individuals. The
influence that a single person may have on the currency is
so minimal, considering the significant number of players in
the market. Further, analysts and brokerage firms do not
have much influence on the trade. As we delve deeper, we
will highlight why it is wrong to rely on TV analysts when
buying stocks. Analysts mostly represent the interests of their

brokerage firms. This puts most stock traders at risk of losing money to scheming analysts who use such opportunities to misguide traders. With that in mind, it is much safer to trade Forex since analysts have vested interests, as is the case with stocks. Unlike stock markets, most Forex analysts have little influence on the exchange rates. Their work is to analyze the market and not influence the currencies.

How Does Forex Trading Work?

There are many ways you can get into Forex trading. In most Forex markets, the trader buys one currency while selling another (exchange) hence the term foreign exchange. Traditionally, traders buy and sell currencies through brokers. However, in modern-day trading, there is an increasing rise in online trading. Online trading makes it easier for traders to participate in direct market analysis and make independent investment choices.

Before we proceed further, we need to look at some of the basic terms used in Forex trading and what they mean. We are going to use the following terms frequently as we proceed in the text.

Base and quote currency: A base currency is the first currency listed in a pair of Forex traded currencies. The second currency is referred to as the quote currency. In Forex markets, currencies are listed in pairs. Further, Forex trading currencies are sold to buy other ones. You can sell the US Dollar to buy the British Pound. The listed price of a Forex pair usually represents the value of a unit of the base currency in the quote currency. For example, if the Forex pair is listed as GBP/USD, the value listed along these figures represents the British Pound's worth in US Dollars. As you can see, each currency is listed in a three-letter code. The first two letters represent the region, while the third letter represents the currency. GBP simply stands for Great British Pound, and USD stands for United States Dollar. The case above simply involves the buying of the British Pound and selling the US Dollar.

We have mentioned that there are four major pairs traded in the Forex market. Well, there are plenty of pairs traded. However, some pairs take up the lion's share of the market. Currently, seven pairs contribute up to 80% of trade volumes in Forex. The four giant pairs include EUR/USD, USD/JPY, GBP/USD, and USD/CHF. These four pairs are currently the dominant forces, determining the trades made in Forex exchange. Just below the giant four pairs follows the EUR/GBP, EUR/CHF, and the GBP/JPY.

Exotics: This is a form of trade in which a currency from an emerging economy is paired against a major currency–for example, USD/MXN or EUR/CZK.

Regional Pairs: This is a trade in which a currency from one region is paired against another currency in the same region. For example, the pairing of Scandinavian currencies EUR/NOK or AUD/SGD.

Short Selling in Forex: In trading, it is possible to profit whichever way the market is moving. It is possible to capitalize if the market is moving upward, downward, or even sideways. If a trader expects that the market will fall, he or she can take advantage of it short selling the asset he or she is trading. To short sell a stock, the trader borrows the stock on margin and sells it. Later the trader will purchase the stock to return it to the lender, buying it on the market at the current price. If the price had fallen, the trader makes a profit.

In Forex, we can apply the same concept of short selling, but it is handled differently from stocks or other financial assets. As we said above, a currency pair involves a base currency and quote currency. This means that if you buy a pair, for example, EUR/USD, you are buying euros and at the same time selling dollars. Vice versa, when you short sell EUR/USD, you are selling euros to buy dollars.

Spread in Forex trading: The spread in Forex terms simply refers to the difference between the selling and buying prices quoted for a Forex pair. In all financial markets, trades are made based on buying and selling. This means that any trade presents two prices. If you want to open a long position,[1] you are expected to buy at the ask price (the lowest price a seller is willing to accept). If you are opening a short position,[2] you are expected to sell at the bid price (the highest price a buyer is willing to accept). The difference between the ask and the bid price is the spread.

A lot in Forex: In Forex trading, currencies are usually traded in lots (batches of currency that help standardize the trade). Lots are large batches that are significant to the trade. For instance, a standard lot is 100,000 units of the base cur-

---

[1]A *long position* is what an investor has purchased when they buy a currency pair, security, or derivative with the expectation that it will rise in value

[2]A *short position* is created when a trader sells a currency pair, security, or derivative first to repurchase it or cover it later at a lower price.

rency. Given that most individual traders cannot afford the value of a lot, say 100,000 pounds, most trades are leveraged. This gives room for small traders to be part of the game. If you want to trade in Forex, you do not necessarily need to have the entire amount to fulfill a lot. As a matter of fact, most platforms allow traders to start their trades with as low as a few hundred dollars. Furthermore, as we are going to see later on in this chapter, it is possible to buy or sell just a little part of a lot (mini lots or micro lots).

Leverage in Forex: Leverage is a way of gaining large profits without trading with large amounts. Using leverage, you only place a deposit on a trade known as a margin. When you trade from a leveraged position, your profit or loss is based on the amount of the trade, not on the amount of the margin. Although leverage can be used to maximize profits, it is also a huge risk and can lead to huge losses. In some trades, the losses can exceed your margin, forcing you to use your assets. Before you start trading using leverage, you must be sure that you can manage your risks properly.

Margin in Forex: As mentioned above, margins are a part of leveraged trading. When you choose to use leverage, you must deposit a certain percentage of the full amount. The margin is the amount you put in place to open and maintain a leveraged trade. Without the margin, you cannot access the trade. Margin requirements may vary depending on the broker and the trade size. In Forex terms, the margin is usually expressed as a percentage of the full position. For instance, if you want to trade a leveraged position on EUR/GBP, you may only be required to deposit, for example, 3.4% of the trade's total value. Once you deposit this amount, the trade is opened and gives you the chance to earn profits from the full amount. For instance, in a position where the trade requires a deposit of £100,000, you may only end up depositing £3400.

A pip in Forex: Pips are units that are used to track movement in a Forex pair. The Forex market is very volatile, while at the same time, currencies may enjoy long-lasting stability. To be able to keep track of the changes, sometimes currencies are broken into tiny units. You may find that the value of a pair stands up to the eighth decimal place. A pip is a one-digit movement in the fourth decimal place of a pair. For instance, if the EUR/USD value is $1.12373 and moves to $1.12383, the change recorded is a pip. Any decimal points shown after the pip are known as fractional pips.

However, the position of a pip is not constant in all currencies. For instance, some currencies have a lower value and may have more decimal positions than others. If the quote currency is listed in a smaller denomination, the pip may be recorded in the second decimal place. For instance, the Japanese Yen is a much weaker currency as compared to the Euro. For EUR/JPY, a pip may be from ¥119.755 to ¥119.765.

What Moves the Forex Market?

The foreign exchange market is made up of currencies from across the world. This makes exchange rate prediction a bit complex. Many factors can influence the movement of currencies, both in local countries and on the international front. Just like other financial markets, Forex trading depends on the forces of supply and demand. Some factors control financial markets, and these forces may also affect Forex trading. Here are some of the key factors that contribute to fluctuations in currency prices.

Central banks: Central banks across different territories mainly control the currency supply. For instance, during quantitative easing, the central bank of a particular country injects more money into the economy. This often leads to a drop in the price of the specific currency due to increased supply.

News reports: News reports are very important in the currency market. Most investors and banks want to put their money in currencies from countries that show positive growth. When there is positive news from a particular region, more investors put their money in such a currency, which may lead to an increase in value for that currency. The news reports include factors such as economic growth, market growth, and political stability, among others. The opposite is also true. If a country receives negative news reports, most investors pull out of its currency, leading to a drastic drop in the currency value. As an investor in Forex, you must also be a friend of news reports. You need to predict political situations and forecast economic growth. Such factors may help you gain more advantage in the trading world.

Market sentiment: Market sentiment is the general feeling among most top traders regarding a specific currency. If traders feel that the currency is headed in a particular direction, they are going to make decisions based on this feeling. In most cases, these decisions drastically change the value of the currency and may lead to an abnormal market movement. It is during such times that expert traders capitalize and realize huge profits.

Crosses

A cross-currency in Forex refers to a trading pair that does not involve the US Dollar. For most Forex pairs, as you may have noticed, the US Dollar is the base or, in some cases, acts as the quote. However, there are pairs where the US currency is not involved in the trade. It is such pairs that are known as crosses in Forex trading. The most common crosses include EUR/JPY and EUR/GBP. These crosses are primarily designed to facilitate trade in countries where the users want to trade without using the US Dollar.

To understand cross-currency, we must go back in history to a time when the financial markets experienced a turnaround (for more insight, see Chapter 5). Post the Second World War, most economies were shaken, and world currencies had experienced a decline in value. At this time, the US currency remained the strongest, and the US economy was the most vibrant. This turn of events meant that the Dollar would serve well as the standard tool for global financial transactions. It followed that individuals who wished to convert two currencies were required to first convert to the US Dollar before changing to the other currency. For instance, if you wanted to convert the British Pound into the Japanese Yen, you had to convert the Pound into the US Dollar first before converting your dollars to the Japanese Yen.

Fast forward several decades down the line, there have been many improvements in global financial markets and shifts in the global economy. Most countries have stabilized their economies and strengthened their currencies. Although the US Dollar still stands out as one of the most stable currencies and acts as the world reserve currency, other currencies also have the strength to influence global trade. Today, cross-currency trades are more common, and many traders do not have to depend on the US Dollar to make trade decisions. For instance, the GBP/JPY cross currency was introduced to facilitate trade in Great Britain and Japan without having to rely on the US Dollar.

There are several advantages of using crosses for traders as well as for individual countries. Given that cross-currency transactions are a normal part of daily trades, they make doing business in Forex markets easier. They are also vital in facilitating international payments. Given that crosses allow an individual to exchange money directly, they make the market cheaper and profitable. Since the trader does not have to convert the currency into the US Dollar first, it means that the trader only has to undergo a single spread. The fact that crosses are now commonly traded has tightened the spread, making it even cheaper to exchange any amount and invest in any economy.

Cross Currency Pairs in Forex Trading

Cross currencies are very vital tools for all Forex traders. Some cross currencies can be used to position traders on particular world events. For instance, in the case of Brexit in the EU, a person could invest in a position anticipating either positive or negative results regarding the Brexit talks. If the investors are required to first trade with the US Dollar before trading in the GBP or the EUR, it would be a more complex trade and may not result in any profits in the long run. In recent years, many traders have been opting for crosses since they seem to hold prospects that the major dollar transactions may not have. For instance, many traders are taking advantage of the carry trade —where they own high-value currency such as the Australian Dollar and short the low-value currency as the Japanese Yen.

In all these efforts, the cross-currency plays a central role in shaping the Forex market. The use of crosses makes it possible for traders worldwide to have more options and flexibility in trading. Although you may still choose to use the traditional methods of converting to the Dollar first, you now have the freedom of trading in currencies you better understand. If you feel that you are more conversant with the situations in the UK, you may choose to only trade GBP and EUR instead of involving the USD.

How to Calculate Pip Value

We have already defined a pip, and as you may have noticed, it is somehow confusing. Pips can be confusing to many traders, especially given that pip is at the fourth decimal place in some pairs, while in other pairs is at the second decimal place. To sort all these issues out, we are going to look at the practical calculation of pip values for certain currencies.

A pip is simply a unit of measurement for a currency movement. In most currency pairs, the pip appears at the fourth decimal place. For example, if the GBP/USD pair moves from 1.2756 to 1.2757, the movement is termed as a one pip movement. If the pair moves to the fifth or sixth decimal places, the following decimal places are referred to as fractional pips. For instance, if there is a movement in the fifth decimal place, e.g., GBP/USD 1.27565 to 1.27566, the movement is referred to as a pipette or a tenth of a pip.

The amount you make in profit or the amount you lose during a trade depends largely on the pip movement. This also depends on the value of the currencies involved and the currency you funded your trade with. You must understand and be able to explain a pip value before you start making Forex investments. Pip values matter in all trades because they help you understand the risk involved. You can't calculate the ideal position size of a trade if you do not know to quantify the value of a pip movement.

Calculating the Pip Value

When you are trading a pair where the USD is listed as the second pair (quote), the pip value remains fixed if your account is funded with US dollars. The value of a pip, in this case, is US $10 for a standard lot of 100,000 units of the currency (US $1 for a mini lot of 10,000 units, or US $0.10 for a micro lot of 1000 units). Such pip values apply to any currency pair where the USD is listed as the quoted value. e.g., the EUR/USD, GBP/USD, AUD/USD, etc.

In cases where the US Dollar is not listed in the second position, you can calculate the pip value by dividing the pip values above with the pair rate. In this case, the pair must contain the US Dollar as the base currency with another currency in the second place. For example, if you want to calculate the pip value for USD/CHF when trading in a US Dollar account, divide US $10 by the USD/CHF rate for a standard lot. Assuming the USD/CHF rate is 0.9352, the pip value in a standard lot is $10/0.9352, which is equal to US $10.69.

The calculation of a pip also depends on the value of the currencies involved. In the case above, all the currencies involved are relatively valuable, and a pip is calculated at the fourth decimal place. However, if the US Dollar was being calculated against the Japanese Yen, for instance, the value would be different. The Japanese Yen pip is calculated at the second decimal place due to its lower value. For a Yen, one pip is equal to 0.01 rather than 0.0001, as is the case with USD and CHF. Therefore, to calculate the lot value in a pair that involves the Japanese Yen as a second pair, the final value has to be multiplied by 100. If the USD/JPY is rated at 107.72, you first have to find the pip value by dividing the USD lot by the exchange rate and then multiply by 100. For a standard lot, the value for a pip in a pair involving a Japanese Yen as a second currency should be US $10/107.72*100, which is equal to US $9.28.

The above calculations are all based on the assumption that you are trading in US dollars. However, some traders prefer trading in other currencies. This may apply to your situation too. Whichever currency you are using to trade, if it is listed as the second currency, then the pip value is fixed. For example, if your account is funded with CAD, any pair that has the CAD as the quoted value, such as USD/CAD, EUR/CAD, etc., enjoys a fixed pip value. The same case applies with the pip value in a standard lot being CAD$10, a mini lot CAD$1, and a micro lot CAD$0.1. To find the value of a pair where the other currency is listed as the first of the pair, simply divide the fixed pip with the currency rate. For example, if the CAD/CHF rate is 0.7366, then the pip value for a standard lot is CAD$10/0.7366, which is equal to CAD$13.57.

In the above cases, we have only considered cases where you want to trade in a currency that funds your account. However, there are situations where you may want to trade in a pair that does not include a currency funding your account. For instance, if your account is funded with USD, you may also want to trade the EUR/GBP. The process of calculating a pip, in this case, is slightly different from the two scenarios above. We have noted from the two previous calculations that the second value is always fixed if you hold an account in that currency. For instance, if you had an account in GBP, then the pip value in a standard lot would be GBP10. However, in this case, GBP is not your account funding; therefore, you must first convert the second value into your account funding currency. If your account is funded with USD, multiply the pip value for a standard lot GBP10 by the GBP/USD rate. For instance, if GBP/USD's rate is 1.2354, then the pip value for a standard lot is GBP10*1.2354. The pip value for EUR/GBP in your account currency is US $12.35. The same case applies to all other currencies. After finding your standard lot value in your account currency, you can make all the other calculations as done above. This process applies to all currencies.

Lots, Mini Lots, Micro Lots

In Forex trading, trades are made in pairs of currencies. In a pair, the first currency is known as the base, and the second currency is the quote. A lot is equivalent to 100,000 units of the base currency. The common units used in Forex include a standard lot, a mini lot, and a micro lot. A mini lot is equivalent to a tenth of the standard lot. In other words, a mini lot is equivalent to 10,000 units of the base currency in a pair. If you are trading with a US Dollar account and trade on a pair with the USD as the quote currency, one pip is equivalent to US $10 for a standard lot and US $1 for a mini lot. Mini lots are very common for Forex mini accounts that are usually opened by Forex brokers.

If you are new to Forex and want to learn to trade, it is recommended that you choose small units of trade. Most beginners start with mini lots as they learn how to trade. Price movements in mini lots have a less significant impact on your trading account, given that the volatility of a position is much less, and traders do not need much money to invest in the trade. Traders with mini lot accounts can start trading with as little as $100 instead of the standard lot accounts where a trader has to invest thousands of dollars to get started.

With that said, mini lots are not just for beginners. Many experienced traders still use mini lots to gain some ground on certain trades. Forex is a game of numbers, and it is much better to trade many different mini lot positions than to risk all your money on a standard lot. Furthermore, advanced traders usually use mini lots to gain greater control over a position. For instance, one trader may prefer to average to a new trend by making multiple small unit positions than making 100,000 units increments at a time.

If you think that lots and mini lots are still a significant risk or you do not have the financial capacity to invest in such terms, you may still break your investments into much smaller proportions. A mini lot can still be broken down into a micro lot.

A micro lot is a tenth of a mini lot. In other words, a micro lot is 1000 units of the base currency. One pip of a pair based in USD is equivalent to US $0.1 when trading a micro lot. Micro lots are much more flexible and pose a lesser risk as compared to mini lots or standard lots.

When starting, most traders tend to try out with micro lots just to find a working strategy. The risk is that most people tend to scale up quickly to the standard lot as soon as they find a good strategy. This is a temptation that you must avoid. One of the biggest mistakes in Forex trading is to try making large profits overnight. As much as a strategy may be promising, you should not be quick to invest all your money in it. It is advisable to scale up gradually.

Another factor to consider is that traders do not behave in the same way when staking large amounts. It is much more difficult to replicate results from the micro lot trades when you jump directly to the larger lots. It is essential to ensure that you understand your trade and can take higher risks before trying to replicate the trade with a higher amount. You have to develop the right mindset before taking higher risks. It is a crucial point.

Sometimes the cost of scaling up may lead to devastating losses, especially if the scale-up does not work to your advantage and if you don't manage your risk correctly. Take your time to analyze your trade strategy and compare all the costs involved in scaling up. If you think that you are in a position to scale up and start making more money, you are free to make a move. However, you must also remember the higher you go, the riskier it gets. As much as scaling up improves your prospects of making huge profits, it also increases your chances of making huge losses.

Bid, Ask, Spread, and Commissions

To be able to make a trade, you must understand these four terms. The term bid mainly refers to the price that a Forex trader is going to pay if he or she wants to sell a particular currency pair. On the other hand, the asking price is the price that the trader is going to pay if he or she wants to buy the currency pair. Both the ask and bid prices are provided in real time and keep on changing. In simple words, you can buy or sell a currency pair within a given price range as long as it is appealing to you.

For example, if the GBP/USD has a bid price of 1.2925, this is the price that the trader is going to get by selling the pair because he or she thinks that the value is going to drop. If the GBP/USD has an ask price of 1.2927, then this is the price that a trader is going to pay to buy the currency pair. As you can see, there is a minimal difference in the bid and ask value. The bid price is always lower than the ask price. The difference between the buy and sell price is what is known as the spread.

Another essential factor to consider in any market is the cost of transactions. You must always calculate how much selling or buying a certain pair is going to cost. One of the most important costs to consider in Forex is, indeed, the commission.

The commission on a trade is the amount of money paid as a service fee to Forex brokers. All traders pay a keen interest in terms of commission, and it may affect the trade significantly. In Forex, commissions vary depending on the type of trade and the broker involved.

If you have had experience with other markets such as equity trading, you probably are more familiar with the concept of commission. Brokers in futures and options are frequently charging commissions on trades at a flat rate on each trade. However, the case is slightly different from the Forex market. In Forex, the commission depends on the broker and the type of dealer. Some of the common charges include fixed commission, variable commission, and per-trade percentage-based commission. All the amounts charged in these commissions are deducted from your profit or your account.

Spread: The Basic Cost of a Trade

The commission in any trade is based on the spread. As we

have seen, all the currency pairs are given at a bid and an ask price. We have also seen that the ask price often tends to be higher than the bid price. Involving a broker in the trade helps you buy your currency at the ask price, the highest value, and sell the same currency at the bid price, the lowest price. The difference between the ask and the bid price makes the spread. A fixed commission is the type of commission that is paid on a fixed spread. For instance, in a trade where there are two or three pips between the ask and the bid price, the trader has to pay a fixed commission. This also depends on the agreement between you and your broker. For example, in a fixed commission trade, if a bid and ask price for EUR/USD is 1.1202/1.1204, the trader may buy the currency at 1.1204 and sell the same currency at 1.1202, which may produce a gain of two pips for the broker. Even if the bid and ask prices move to 1.1204/08, the broker will charge the same two pip difference as the commission per unit bought and sold.

The bid and ask prices are always changing, depending on the financial market performances and other factors we have looked at above. The prices can change according to the demand and supply of a certain currency. For example, if the EUR/USD may first appear with a bid and ask spread of two pips, say 1.1220/1.1222, after just a few minutes or seconds, this value can change depending on the market forces. The bid/ask prices for the above pair could change to three pips 1.1232/1.1235. In such cases, the spread widens because there is less liquidity in the market or more volatility. In some instances, a significant news event might cause a drastic shift in the bid and ask prices, increase volatility, and provoke abnormal price changes.

On the other hand, a percentage-based commission is only

a small percentage that is accounted for within the spread. In such a case, the broker is entitled to an agreed percentage, which may only be equal to a fraction of a pip. The remaining amount is left for the market maker whom the broker is working for. This type of commission is ok for traders and may allow them to make profits by paying lower costs.

Swaps

If you are a new Forex trader or if you are just starting, you may have a bit of a problem describing what a swap is. Well, while it's not mandatory to understand swaps, knowing what they are and how they operate may give you an edge in your trade.

A swap is an interest that is paid when a trader holds a position overnight. Usually, a trader is required to make a delivery of currency purchased within two days from the transaction date. However, in some instances, traders may extend the settlement period by a day. In this case, the trader has to simultaneously close the trade at the rate and reenter the new opening position at the new rate for the next trading day (rollover).

Every trade involves currency borrowing. In order to trade, the Forex trader borrows a currency from one country to buy the currency of another country. The borrowing generates interest, either owed or paid. This is a swap.

Swaps are important to know because owning a currency is a strategy used to gain interest. This strategy is called "carry trade." To make sure that they gain interest, traders take a long position in a high-yielding currency compared to the currency used in making the purchase. In the case that the borrowed currency outperforms the currency used in purchasing, the trader will earn the interest.

In most cases, it is advisable to close your trade at the end of the day, usually 5:00 p.m. in your local time, depending on your location. On the other hand, you may think that a currency is going to perform better overnight. In this case, you may use a swap to prolong the trade and increase your chances of making more money from it.

If you want to have success in trading Forex, you must understand how swaps operate and how they may impact your income. In any instance, a swap fee is incurred in any trade where the position is kept overnight. The fee for the swap is calculated by determining the difference between the two currencies being traded. This is often conditioned on whether the trade is long or short. Interest rates can be negative or positive in a swap trade, depending on whether the trader is borrowing or lending the higher-yielding currency.

Type of Orders

The word order, as used in Forex, is to mean "enter or exit a trade." In other words, we are looking at the types of commands a person can use to execute a trade. Knowing the type of orders that your Forex broker accepts is very important. There are some basic orders that most brokers accept. However, there are certain orders that your Forex broker may not be allowed to process. Here are the main types of orders and what they mean:

Market order: This mainly refers to an order to either buy or sell at the best value. For instance, if the bid price for EUR/USD is 1.1202 and the ask price is 1.1204, if you want to buy the pair, it is going to be sold to you at the ask price. To process this order, you must click buy, and the trading platform will immediately process the order at that price. This process is similar to online shopping. If you have shopped on Amazon, just think of the market order as the one-click ordering process. If you like the currency price, you click, and immediately, the currency is yours. However, this does not guarantee that you will be able to purchase all the pairs at the listed price. Depending on the market forces, there may be differences in the prices you see compared to the price you buy. This is because the market prices can change in microseconds.

Limit Entry Order: A limit entry is an order that a trader places in order to buy below or sell above the market price. For instance, if you are trading EUR/USD and it is currently trading at 1.1204, you may want to wait until the price hits 1.1224 before you sell. In this case, either you may choose to stay in front of your screen and wait for the trade to reach the target value, or you can set a sell limit order of 1.1224. This gives you the freedom to leave your screen and do other things while you wait for the price to rise to your expected value. If the graph finally reaches the 1.1224 targets, the trading platform automatically executes the order to sell or buy. This is a good strategy that may help you make a profit while you are busy doing other activities, but it also involves risks. Assuming that you set a selling price at 1.1224 and leave the system to execute the order, in case the value keeps rising to 1.1264, you are likely to miss a big profit in your absence.

Stop-Loss Order: This is a type of order which a trader makes to stop the possible occurrence of a loss. In a long position, you can make a sell stop order to reduce the losses expected. In a short position, you can make a buy stop order to prevent buying into a losing pair. This order remains in place until the position is liquidated. For example, if you chose to long buy EUR/USD at 1.1220, you may choose to limit your potential loss by setting your Stop-Loss Order at 1.1180. In this trade, you are anticipating the prices to keep on rising. However, assuming that you were all wrong and the EUR/USD drops to 1.1180 instead of moving up as you expected, the platform automatically sells the pair and stop further losses. Stop-loss orders are essential and can be used if you do not want to risk too much or do not want to sit in front of your computer for hours waiting to see the movement of prices. You can set a stop-loss order so that you can attend to other activities within the day. Such orders also prevent losses that may arise from fast-moving positions that you may not have total control over.

Trailing Stop: A trailing stop order is an order that moves with the price as it fluctuates. For instance, if you choose to short USD/JPY at 111.90 with a stop order at -20 pips, it means that your original stop price is at 112.10. In case the price goes down and hits 111.70, then the trailing stop now would be at 111.90. However, it is important to remember that the stop remains at this level, even if the price goes up again. For instance, in the example above, the trailing stop of 20 pips would remain live as long as the prices do not move against you by 20 pips. If the USD/JPY moves, instead, to 111.50, then the stop order would move to 111.70. As soon as the market price coincides with the trailing stop order price, you can close your position at the best value possible.

Good-Till-Canceled (GTC): A Good-Till-Canceled order is an order in which you have total control. A good till order remains active until you choose to cancel it. Your broker cannot cancel such an order unless you do it yourself. Therefore, it is your responsibility to remember the order and close it if you do not wish to proceed with the trade.

Good for the Day (GFD): A GFD order is an order that remains active until the close of the day. Given that Forex trading is a 24-hour business, a GFD means that the trade has to close at 5:00 P.M. EST when the market closes in the US. This is specifically for US traders; you have to counter-check with your local time. In most areas, the closing time is between 4:00 P.M. and 5:00 P.M. local time.

One-Cancels-the-Other (OCO): As the name suggests, this type of order has two open orders at the same time. The two orders may include entry and/or stop-loss orders. The two orders are placed above and below the current price. In this case, when one order is executed, the other one is automatically canceled. For instance, EUR/USD is 1.1220, and you decide to buy if the price goes to 1.1270. At the same time, you want to sell if the price goes below 1.1170. The scenario may play out that 1.1270 is reached, and the buy order is executed; then, the 1.1170 sell order is automatically canceled.

One-Triggers-the-Other: An OTO is the exact opposite of the OCO. In OTO, one order triggers the execution of another. An OTO is used to set the take-profit and stop-loss orders even before you get into a trade. For instance, if the USD/CHF is trading at 0.9855 and you want to go short on this currency pair but you want to position your trade below this value, you may set up a sell limit order at 0.9845. Unfortunately, you may not have an entire week to watch over the price fluctuations to see if your predictions come to pass. The best way to ensure that you are in place to execute the trade is to set an OTO. Set your sell limit order at 0.9845 in this case and also set a

buy limit at 0.9745 as a take-profit. If you are not sure you are
going to be around to monitor the progress, you may also set
a stop-loss order at 0.9945. In this trade, both the stop-loss
and the take-profit order may only be activated if the value
of 0.9845 is triggered. Therefore, the entire trade depends on
one position being triggered.

You should not attempt Forex trading before you gain a
basic understanding of the above orders. These orders are vital
in helping Forex traders place trade commands and safeguard
their money by stopping a trade when necessary. All these
factors depend on your understanding of the orders. The
basic rule for beginners in Forex trading is KISS (Keep It
Simple, Stupid). In other words, do not try complicating your
trades or choosing complex positions. You can make money
by understanding how simple orders work and executing them
at the right time.

There is always the option to trade with a demo version
(so-called paper trading) before you start live trading. It is
recommended to learn about these orders and other trading
techniques on the demo version. This gives you a real opportunity to learn more about the platform and to understand how
the trade operates. After trading successfully on the demo
version, you can deposit some money and advance to the next
step.

Margin

Margin is the good faith deposit that a trader has to put up
as collateral to start a trade. It is the amount of money that
traders need in their account to be able to open a new position.
The margin is usually expressed as a percentage of the trade
size. The difference between the full trade value and the margin
is referred to as the borrowed amount since it is borrowed from

the broker. For example, in a case where the standard lot is equivalent to $10,000, if the margin required is 3.33%, the trader may only deposit $333 to be able to participate in such a trade.

Open/Close Hours for Different Markets

The concept of opening and closing times is very clear in commodity trading. Most people who have traded in stocks and commodities fail to understand the operations of the Forex market in terms of time. To be able to understand the time of opening and closing, you must first conceptualize the trading system. Unlike commodities, which are traded physically at the trade center, Forex is traded online through Electronic Communication Networks (ECNs). The trade happens in a variety of markets across the globe.

Forex is a 24-hour business in most parts of the world. The trading starts at 5:00 P.M. EST on Sunday to Friday, 4:00 P.M. EST in the United States. This time correlates with the trading hours in other localities. The time difference based on different locations across the world means that there is a trading center open at any given time. This means that international traders online can keep on trading even if the local trading center is closed.

There are three key trading regions in the world, and they open in the order of their locations. Given that they all open at 5:00 P.M. Sunday and close at 4:00 P.M. Friday, they have to follow a specific order to ensure constant business continuity at all times. Forex first opens in Australia and Asia regions, then followed by Europe, and finally North America. The North American Market sets the pace for the other trading platforms. The time difference between the North American and Australian regions provides a period of up to twenty-four hours between the closing and opening of the sessions.

Another factor contributing to the 24-hour business is that currencies are needed around the clock to facilitate trade in the world. This means that central banks rely on Forex trade to ensure a continuous flow of foreign exchange. In 1971, the fixed currency market ceased to exist, forcing all central banks to turn to Forex markets for a continuous flow of money through-out the world. If the Forex market stops for an instant, there may be far-reaching effects in the economies that rely on the exchange for business's continuous transaction.

What Makes 24-Hour Trading Possible?

The main reason why 24-hour trading is possible is that it happens online. Traders are not limited to a specific physical location. Further, the international time zones play a role in ensuring that there is a time overlap between the opening and the closing of various trade centers.

When we say that the Dollar closed at a certain rate, it simply means that it closed at that rate in that specific country. The US Dollar can only close at a specific rate in the US. However, the currency continues to be traded in different markets throughout the world. Unlike securities, Forex trading never comes to an end at any given point. Those who are experts in trading securities are used to business closure every day. Do not pressure yourself so much trying to relate securities to Forex. If you are introducing yourself to Forex from securities, you need to let go of some knowledge you brought in and start learning new ways of doing business.

Economic Calendar and Main Indicators

The Forex economic calendar is one of the most important trading tools that every Forex trader must use. If you are not conversant with the economic calendar, you may end up losing money in huge sums. The economic calendar dictates the strength of each currency and, as a result, affects the pricing of currency pairs.

The calendar mainly contains information on existing, past, and upcoming economic events that may affect certain currencies' strength (for more insight, see Chapter 6). To understand how the calendar operates, you must first conceptualize the factors that affect a currency's strength. Each currency traded in Forex is a representation of the economic, political, and social stability of a country. In essence, if any country experiences social, political, or economic instability, the currency of that country is likely to lose strength. In this light, any changes to the economic indicators of a nation are likely to change the strength of the currency either positively or negatively. Given that each pair consists of two currencies representing two different economies, the pair represents the balance of economic operations between the two countries.

A good example would be the EUR/USD. This pair is one of the most traded pairs for the simple reason that the two economies they represent enjoy economic stability. The Euro is the currency used in the Euro Zone, while the USD is the currency used in the United States of America. If you are trading EUR/USD, you must pay attention to the economic and political events in the two countries. Any significant economic, political, or social occurrence in the Eurozone or in the US may lead to significant changes in the EUR/USD pair rates. If you expect political unrest in the US, you should know that the USD's value is likely to be affected.

There are plenty of events on the Forex economic calendar, all of which tend to indicate the right time to make certain investment choices. Some of the events have a huge economic impact, while others are minor. As a trader, you do not have to focus on all the events on the calendar. Your work is to determine the events that are likely to cause volatility in the market (for more insight, go to the A Free Gift for You page at the end of this book). Such events give you the strength to plan your investment choices in advance.

Platform: MT4/MT5

As we have already established, Forex trading happens over a platform. The platform of trade allows you to conduct your orders and hence make profits or losses. MetaQuotes Software, popularly known as Meta Trader, is the leading software in the market that facilitates Forex trading. Meta Trader allows traders to view live charts of the Forex market and make informed decisions based on the trends.

MetaQuotes Software Corp, the company behind the software, was established in the year 2000. Since then, it has grown to become one of the leading software manufacturers for the financial markets. They have developed complex software such as the Meta Trader and even simple chart view platforms. The Meta Trader has been developed over the years and now is currently running on two versions: the Meta Trader 4 and Meta Trader 5. These are the leading software used in Forex trading globally and are popularly known as MT4 and MT5, respectively.

Both options are very efficient and provide a variety of tools for brokers and traders. Most traders use either the MT4 or MT5, which help provide a variety of options for traders. These software versions provide the chance for traders to view the live trading charts and prices. The software also allows traders to open accounts, manage them, and place orders. With that said, there are a few differences between the MT4 and MT5 that traders must understand. Before you start trading, you should consider these factors.

Factors to Consider

The MT4 was released in July 2005 and has been reserved as a simple trading platform, mostly used by the online retail Forex market. On the other hand, the MT5 was released in 2010, providing an all-in-one state-of-the-art platform for multi-asset trading.

Mobility: By using the mobile version of the software offered through both MT4 and MT5, you are able to make transactions on the go via Android and iOS apps. This provides the convenience of trading twenty-four hours a day anywhere you are in the world.

The platforms are friendlier, providing functional charts and a full set of trading orders. You can also use popular analytical tools, which help you to monitor your accounts and financial instruments.

Analytics: When it comes to analytical aspects, both the MT4 and MT5 are effective in ensuring that you get the right information. Both platforms provide a custom platform that suits an individual trader.

- The MT5 is much-advanced when it comes to displaying interactive time frames. The MT4 provides only nine interactive time frames to choose from, while the MT5 boasts of whooping twenty-one time frames.
- The MT4 platform boasts of thirty built-in indicators, while the MT5 boasts of thirty-eight built-in technical in-

dicators. The MT5 provides several additions for drawing tools, such as the Elliot wave drawing and the Fibonacci studies.

■ Both MT4 and MT5 provide alert functions, including audio notifications. They also provide the latest financial news from across the globe, which works well for those who trade in several options. MT5 economic calendar notifies traders when important macroeconomic news is about to break out.

■ The MT5 platform provides the depth of market data (DOM), which allows traders to view where the offers are priced across the Forex market.

Algorithmic trading: The trading algorithm simply refers to the trading platform's systematic assistance in terms of automation. Both MT4 and MT5 provide trading robots that help automate the process of trading.

■ Both MT4 and MT5 offer sophisticated automation that can help you as a trader make informed choices and execute your trades better. The MT4 platform uses MetaQuotes Language 4 (MQL4) programming to address client needs and concerns. On the other hand, MT5 uses MetaQuotes Language 5 (MQL5) for the same purposes. Both languages are efficient enough, although each suffers a few inconsistencies that may be addressed by support teams.

■ To benefit from either MQL4 or MQL5, the traders have to learn and understand the language. This may help you generate any type of advice or assistance from the system. Further, being able to communicate with the system in the languages provided makes it possible for you to automate trade and create indicators.

- It is important to note that programs that are compatible with MQL4 are usually not compatible with the MQL5 system.

- MQL5 is the most used and is viewed to be easier to use than the MQL4. It also provides an easy step-by-step process for completing trading operations, which is different from MQL4, which requires that the trader goes through several steps before completing an operation.

Trading and orders: We have already looked at the various trading orders and established that they are an integral part of Forex trading. If you cannot get your trading orders right, the chances are that you might go through a lot of trouble. Both MT4 and MT5 have a similar execution mode for the orders placed. The platforms provide either instant execution, execution by market, or execution on request. However, the MT5 platform offers the extra advantage of exchange execution. In exchange execution, orders can be sent to an external trading system for execution.

In terms of pending orders at a predefined price, the MT4 platform offers four types of orders (buy limit, buy stop, sell limit, sell stop). On the other hand, the MT5 offers up to six orders, including the buy-sell stop limit.

2 Main Technical Analysis Instruments

Getting to know the basics of Forex trading before you start interpreting the graphs is an essential aspect of trading. You must understand the commonly used Forex terms as outlined in the previous chapter and be in a position to interpret a simple Forex chart. You should also be able to relate to Forex news and adjust according to the events in the market that control it. When you start trading for the first time, it is better to have a person with a level of experience who can assist you. Of course, you may also learn some important aspects by watching tutorials and reading books. However, you must also be careful not to get information from people who only want your money.

There are many types of charts, and your ability to analyze such charts will give you room for success in Forex. There are three types of charts that you must be able to read and interpret if you wish to make any progress as a Forex trader: candlestick[1], bar, and line charts. Each of these charts is

---

[1]A candlestick is a way of representing prices in technical analysis. It originated in the 18th century from Japanese rice traders. Each candlestick represents one period (one day, one hour, 4 hours, and so on, depending on the chosen timeframe). Each candlestick displays all four

important and relevant at specific points on the graph.

If you wish to gain success in Forex, you have to look for a platform that offers more than just live charts and figures. As you advance in trading, you realize that the data you get and the tools you have available for analyzing the data are vital in making good trade decisions. In this chapter, we will be looking at some of the essential features and tools that you should expect from a trading platform and how to determine if a platform is okay for you.

Trend Lines

Trend lines are the most common tool used in the technical analysis of a Forex graph. If you can master how to analyze and draw your trend line, you are probably going to make more profits than losses as a trader. Trend lines are usually the most accurate prediction of a trend and can be drawn on any type of graph. By definition, the trend line is a line connecting two or more highs or two or more lows on a currency pair graph, as seen in the image in figure 2.1. In the most basic form, a trend line indicating an uptrend (uptrend line) is drawn along the most obvious bottom points in the graph. On the other hand, a downtrend line is drawn along the most recognizable top points (see figure 2.1). If you want to draw a trend line, you must first locate at least two significant points, either tops or bottoms. The points you choose should be considerably spaced to allow a significant portion of the graph to be within the area of the trend line. Connect the two (or three) points, and you get a trend line. Trend lines help to identify the trend.

essential pieces of information for a specific period: the high, low, open, and close. When the close is higher than the open, we have a bullish candlestick, and it is generally white or green. When the close is lower than the open, we have a bearish candlestick, and it is generally black or red.

Figure 2.1: *Trend line in a downtrend (EUR/USD, h4 time frame) (Created with MT4. ©Metaquotes Software Corp.)*

There are three types of trends:

1. Uptrend
2. Downtrend
3. Sideways trend

When it comes to drawing trends, you must keep in mind that not all lines connecting points on a graph can be termed as trends. It is the choice of the points used that makes a trend valid. Drawing your trend line without careful consideration of the most critical peaks or bottoms may lead to a misleading analysis. If you draw your line in the wrong manner, you may end up losing your money by bidding in the wrong direction. It takes at least three bottoms or tops to confirm a trend. You may connect two points, but they end up being entirely outside the line with other points on the curve. To confirm that your trend line is significant, it should connect at least three points on the line of interest. A trend line becomes even stronger and more accurate the more times it is tested. As you can see in figure 2.1, usually, during a trend, the price retraces to the trend line before continuing the down or uptrend. If prices violate the trend line, it is a signal that the trend is pausing or reversing.

One of the biggest mistakes made by most traders is to force the position of a trend line. If you realize that a certain pair is giving out irregular graphs and that it is not possible to predict the direction of the trend, do not try to force a trend line to fit. There are some instances where the trade may be irregular due to abnormal market influence. If external forces infiltrate the market, it becomes hard to predict the direction of the trend. The graph may experience irregular movements making it impossible to connect two valid points within a specific time frame. If this is the case, you should relax and avoid forcing the points to connect. If you force a trend to occur, you may only end up losing money in poor-trade decisions.

The best choice you can make is to trade in favor of the trend to have more chances to end up in a profitable trade. Always remember that "the trend is your friend!"

Support and Resistance

The concept of support and resistance forms the foundation upon which most Forex traders operate. In simple terms, support indicates areas of the graph where an uptrend is likely to ensue. Forex traders seek to buy at, or near, a level of prices where there is a potential for an uptrend. If you are buying USD/EUR at 1.1000, you are expecting to sell the same at a higher rate, say 1.1080. When you buy this pair at this value, a support area gives you more chances of an increase in prices according to the overall look of the graph. Resistance, on the other hand, refers to areas of the graph where there is a significant potential for a downward trend. These are the areas of maximum potential gain within the period of trade according to your anticipation. In the resistance areas, most people are likely to sell. Selling at the resistance points gives you high chances to gain a profit. There is a general term used in the trading business, "buy low and sell high."This principle is indeed what people use to operate in all types of business. The aim is to buy low and sell at the highest possible price to maximize profits in an upward trend. Vice versa, in a downward trend, we want to "sell high and buy back low."

To help quantify or estimate the lows and highs, we use graphical representations of price trends for a certain pair. The area where the prices stop after an upward trend is known as the resistance level. Once the upward trend stops, the prices immediately take a downward trend. The areas where the downward trend stops are known as the support level.

The chart in figure 2.2 is a perfect depiction of support and resistance levels in a trade. As you can see from the graph, in a upward trend traders prefer to buy at support and make their profits at the next resistance level. The main reason why traders chose to enter a trade at or near areas of support or resistance is that it reduces the risk significantly. Think of the resistance level as the maximum possible price for the pair.

A person selling at resistance is selling at the maximum possible price within a specific time frame. In the same manner, think of support as the lowest possible price for a pair. A person buying at support is buying at the lowest possible price within the time period. Of course, Forex trading is much more complicated when you look at it in detail. For instance, the fact that support prices stand at the lowest possible level is relative to your analytical interpretation. The lowest price level of support or the highest price level of resistance can only be termed the lowest or highest possible at that particular time

Figure 2.2: *Support and resistance levels in an uptrend (source:*
www.dailyfx.com)

or within a specific time frame. However, things are bound to
change, and the point initially viewed as the lowest possible
point may easily turn out to be the highest possible point after
some time.

Both areas of support and resistance are used as entry
points and profit targets. An area of significant resistance
provides the right entry point for a downtrend. The next area
of support, as anticipated by the trader, can be the point of
return. On the other hand, in an uptrend, levels of significant
support provide ideal entry points. They clearly show countertrend seller exhaustion at the point when buyers return to be
dominant. The next level of resistance can be used as a target
area because it is an area where sellers return to be dominant.
Support and resistance can also be used as a breakout entry
area if the price closes below support or above resistance (see
Chapter 3 for more insights).

You need to determine the support and choose to buy in
an uptrend or sell at resistance on a downtrend in a regular

market. But if the market has been influenced by an external force, the decision to buy or sell may not be dependent on this kind of analysis. Sometimes a political or economic event may lead to an abnormal market, which does not depend on the laws of demand and supply. In such a case, the decision to buy or sell should be made based on personal analysis of the situation.

Very often, in this type of market, it is better not to trade and wait until the situation gets clear.

A support or resistance point is not just a random point where the price automatically turns up or down. Many analytical factors determine the movement of prices. Such factors can determine whether the turnaround happens or if the trend is prolonged. Some traders choose to sell their pair and regret considering the potential they had to push the prices even further. These possible turnaround points should only act as indicators and should be critically analyzed in relation to the trend. It is also vital to note that trends change. As much as you may want to use the turning points to make a trade decision, you should be careful not to decide to buy at the point where you are supposed to sell, and vice versa.

The support and resistance points are caused by consequential trading choices. As already established above, the forces of demand and supply determine the prices of currencies. At the same time, some traders take long positions while others make short trades. The investment choices made by each trader play a significant role in determining the overall pricing of currency pairs and in ensuring that the price keeps moving up and down.

In support and resistance levels, the demand and the supply are in equilibrium. That is why prices stop falling in the support area and stop rising in the resistance area. Furthermore, as in the past, in these points, supply and demand were balanced (equilibrium), and the market tends to remember it in the future.

Support and resistance levels are significant if they are touched at least three times or more by prices in the graphs (see figure 2.3). The more times, the more significant the level is.These levels are sensitive prices where the market reacts, selling or buying big volumes causing the prices to change direction.

If we consider higher time frames than hourly or daily (like weekly or monthly), these levels of prices are even more significant because they are long term significant price points. Consider also that a level of resistance can become a level of support, and vice versa.

Figure 2.3: *Example of resistance and support levels (USD/JPY, weekly time frame) (Created with MT4. ©Metaquotes Software Corp.)*

Figure 2.4: *Example of 50 and 14-period Moving Average (USD/CAD, hourly time frame) (Created with MT4. ©Metaquotes Software Corp.)*

Moving Average

The moving average is an indicator used to show the average closing price of a market within a given period of time. Most traders rely on the moving average to make trade decisions since it works as an indicator of the current market momentum. If a certain pair has been increasing with an average of 0.001 per hour, the momentum may continue for a few more hours before there is a shift.

Two types of moving averages are recognized and are commonly used in Forex: the Simple Moving Average (SMA) and the Exponential Moving Average (EMA). The SMA does not give any weight to the data within the trend, while the EMA gives weight to the averages within a specific data set, including current prices.

The moving average is one of the most important technical analysis tools. Almost all charts must provide a moving average of some sort, mostly EMA and SMA. The SMA is the average of all the data points within the series divided by the number of points. If you have ten consecutive data points, you can add them up and divide them by ten to get the simple moving average (SMA). The SMA is often criticized for its direct approach to the analysis of the graph. Analysts argue that SMA contains all the points within a data set that have equal weight within the SMA, making it unrealistic to reflect the current market trend. For instance, if the market has been dropping by 0.002 and then it turns around and starts rising by 0.002, for an equal amount of time, the simple moving average indicates that the market is not showing any change at the current level, which is not true. Although there has been a shift from negative to positive with an equal proportion, this is not reflected at all in the indicator.

The EMA was specifically developed to correct the inconsistencies brought about by the SMA. The EMA tends to give more weight to recent prices, making it more realistic and sensitive to current market prices. To calculate the SMA and the EMA, follow these simple mathematical formulas.

Simple Moving Average:

$$SMA = \frac{A1 + A2 + \ldots An}{n}$$

A = each data point
n = number of data point

For instance, if you want to calculate the SMA for a 5-day period, in which case you are given the closing prices of each day, you have to add the closing prices for the five days and then divide them by 5.

Calculation for the Exponential Moving Average:

$$EMA_t = EMA_{t-1} + s \cdot (P_t - EMA_{t-1})$$

EMA_t= exponential moving average
P_t = Value today
s = smoothing factor.

Steps for calculating EMA:
1. First, calculate the SMA for the particular time frame (SMA equal EMA at time 0);
2. Calculate the coefficient for weighting the EMA by using the following formula: $2/(n+1)$ where n = nuber of preiods:
3. Now use the smoothing factor and combine it with the previous SMA to get the EMA.

What Is the Importance of Moving Average?
Most traders fail to grasp the importance of the moving average and only look at it as a decoration for the chart. However, if you are keen on analyzing the market, you must realize that the moving average is the one sure way of making investment decisions that are based on facts and not impulse. The moving average is the indicator of the market direction within a defined period. It means that by basing your investments on the moving average, you are in a position to eliminate fluctuations caused by momentary changes in the market.

Since the moving average is a representation of the overall closing market prices over a specific number of days (or hours, minutes, months, or weeks), it helps traders to avoid inconsistencies that may be due to specific events within a given period.

Another significant benefit of the moving average is that it can be customized. You may choose to calculate the moving average for the last month, or you may choose to calculate for the last three days. In this manner, a trader is in a position to choose a time period that is most relevant to the kind of investment he or she wants to make. For instance, if a specific pair had been losing by two pips in the last seven days, and then it starts raising for three days, you may choose to eliminate the initial seven days from your calculations and only focus on the gaining days. In simple terms, you can calculate the average within a reasonable period of time that accurately represents your needs and your intentions in the market. If you know what you want and how to achieve it, it is simple and straightforward. You can use the moving average calculation to get a glimpse of what to expect for the next few days or weeks.

We have established that the moving average is very important, and a trader can use it in three key ways:

- To determine and predict the direction of a market trend (short and long term);
- To identify or determine support and resistance points;
- To determine entry and exit signals.

Although you may use the MA for many purposes, most traders use the moving average to determine the trend and to indicate the support and resistance points. In determining the direction of trends, if prices are above one or more moving averages, it is an indication of an uptrend. If prices are below one or more moving averages, it is an indication of a downtrend.

A moving average's accuracy in determining an uptrend or a downtrend depends on the formula of calculations and the data sets considered within the chosen time period. For instance, if you are calculating a moving average for the past ten days that have been showing a decline in prices, a significant rise in prices on the tenth day may have little impact on the moving average. For this reason, traders need to learn to use the EMA instead of the SMA when doing such calculations. The EMA provides a more realistic indicator in determining the market's direction for the short and medium-term.

Moving averages can also help identify support and resistance points when you are in a position to spot upward and downward trends. If the price is trading just below the moving average, the MA becomes a resistance point. If the price is above the moving average, the MA becomes a support point.

If a trader recognizes that the prices have moved below the moving average and are deepening further below the MA, going very far from it, they may spot it as an opportunity to buy. When the prices moved above the moving average, and they go very further above, it is an opportunity to sell. When you buy or sell at these levels (very far from a MA), you have high chances that the trend will shift and that prices will start coming back to the MA, which becomes a support or resistance point. This kind of movement is very common, and it is known as "return to the mean".

Lastly, moving averages also indicate changes in prices and are used as a market entry or exit signal. When the prices, while increasing, cross the moving average, it is a bullish signal, where most traders prefer buying. On the other hand, if prices cross the moving average while decreasing, it would be a bearish signal, and most traders would prefer selling.

Making Use of Multiple Moving Averages

It is possible to have more than a single moving average on the same chart. This can be achieved by either calculating the average over different time periods or using both EMA and SMA on the same chart. Either way, providing more than a single moving average puts you in an advantageous position. To those who are new to Forex, an attempt to use multiple moving averages may be confusing. However, it is recommended to test the market by drawing more than one moving average. When you use multiple moving averages, you are in a position to determine both short and long-term trends. One currency pair may be on an upward trend within a period of one month, but it may also experience a deep drop within two or three days in the same month. If you use your monthly average to trade the pair during the three days of a downward trend, you may lose. However, if you use a short-term MA to calculate the direction for the short-term period, you have higher probabilities to gain.

When you use multiple moving averages, there are situations where the lines might cross. At the point where the averages cross, they form what is known as the "golden cross,"forming a bullish pattern and as a "death cross,"forming a bearish pattern.

The golden cross is formed in case the short-term moving average crosses above the long-term moving average. For instance, if a 20-day moving average crosses above a 50-day moving average, the golden cross is formed. Vice versa, if the short-term moving average crosses below the long-term moving average, then a death cross is formed. At the same time, if you are into a trade (long or short), a death cross or a golden cross can be an indicator that you should close the trade.

Relative Strength Index (RSI) and Stochastic

An **oscillating indicator** is a term used in the trading world to mean indicators that vary between two values on a graph. Commonly known as oscillators, oscillating indicators show if a pair has been overbought or oversold. Oscillators are usually plotted on a histogram. They are more commonly used as banded oscillators, where the lines move between bands, indicating extreme prices (oversold and overbought).

When prices are above the upper band, it is an indication to sell. Vice versa, when prices are below the lower band, it is an indication to buy.

Relative strength index and stochastic oscillator are oscillating indicators usually used to forecast the trends in a market, especially in sideways trending markets, spotting the possible changes in direction. These indicators lose a lot of their effectiveness in an uptrend or downtrend because they can stay in the overbought or oversold area for a long time. Furthermore, in a low time frame (usually lower than the hourly time frame or even daily), oscillators become very reactive and less informative, giving many false signals.

Although the relative strength index and the stochastic oscillator are both essential analytical tools and work to provide the same solution for traders, these two indicators operate on two independent theories. The relative strength index is the most popular.

Relative Strength Index

J. Welles Wilder, one of the most successful traders of our era,

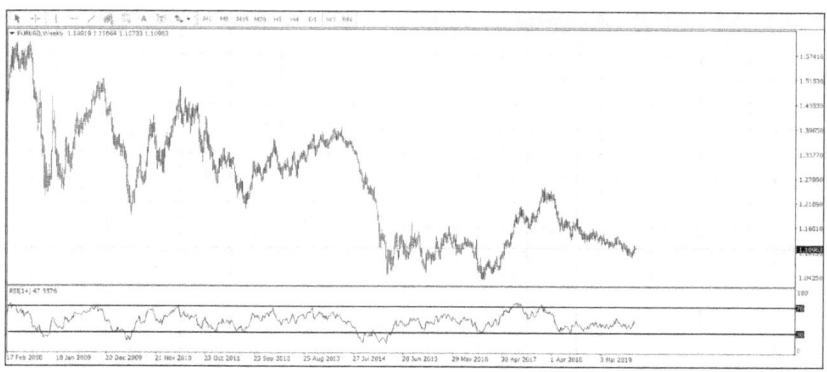

Figure 2.5: *Example of 14-period RSI (EUR/USD, weekly time frame) (Created with MT4. ©Metaquotes Software Corp.)*

developed the RSI indicator after comparing recent gains to recent losses in a market. The RSI indicator mainly focuses on tracking the overbought and oversold levels of the prices and, as a result, provides the value for the velocity of the movements. The RSI is a line on a graph that moves in between two extremes, and it is recorded in percentage. RSI is usually plotted underneath the price chart (see figure 2.5). In an RSI indicator chart, the midpoint is usually 50, and in case the RSI value goes above 70, the currency pair is considered to be overbought. At the same time, the pair is considered oversold if the RSI level goes below 30.

The RSI formula divides the overall number of positive changes in the last n periods by the total of negative changes. That is why RSI measures the velocity of the price movement.

As we said in the moving average section, prices can move away from the average value, until a certain distance, before going back to the mean. Usually, fast movements of prices (up or down) happen in a condition of oversold or overbought. The RSI slope and values are directly correlated to the velocity and the magnitude of the price movement: the more rapid and

Figure 2.6: *Example 20-period Stochastic (EUR/USD, H4 time frame) (Created with MT4. ©Metaquotes Software Corp.)*

significant is the price movement, the steeper is the RSI, and the more extreme are its values.

Stochastic Oscillator

Stochastic oscillators are momentum indicators that were created by George Lane. This type of indicator mainly measures the position of the present price in a range of prices within the trading period of choice, and it is very useful in identifying the tops and the bottoms in prices.

The stochastic oscillator operates on the theory that the closing prices should be the closest to the trend direction. According to Lane, prices are likely to close near the highs of the price range in an uptrending market and near the lows in a downtrending market. If in an uptrend or downtrend, prices close within the price range in a specified period of time, it means that the trend is getting weaker.

Although this theory has been widely criticized, it is also widely accepted and used by many traders. Just like the RSI, the stochastic values are plotted in percentages, ranging from 0 to 100. However, in this case, the overbought indication starts when the value is above 80 and not 70, as is the case with RSI. When the value is below 20, the indicator is in an oversold area. The stochastic oscillator chart usually contains two lines, one indicating the value of the oscillator of the chosen trade period and the other indicating the simple moving average of the indicator. The crossing of these two lines gives a signal of change in price direction. Furthermore, any intersection between these lines and the 80–20 levels is a reinforcement of the signal of a reversal.

3 Main Strategies and Money Management

So far, we have looked at some of the essential definitions in the Forex world. We have also looked at some of the available analysis tools and how you can use the charts to make the right trade decisions. While these factors are important and useful to every trader, having knowledge does not always equate to success as a Forex trader. For you to succeed, you must find a profitable strategy and turn your knowledge into actual trade actions. In this chapter, we move a notch higher in our quest to find the hidden secrets of Forex trading.

Seasoned investors are well aware of the need for a clear trading strategy. Novice investors are generally guilty of entering the markets without a sound strategy that can facilitate their actions when looking to invest. This can be a crucial mistake –naturally, mistakes when investing lead to losses.

This is why all investors need to develop their own strategy so that they know how to act in any given circumstance. In addition, a solid investment strategy is a great way of taking the guesswork out of investing. This implies that a good strategy is practically half of the ground that investors need to make up when looking to get started in their trading endeavors.

Every strategy will have some profit and some losses. It is not possible to eliminate losses in trading. This is a hard truth about trading that you must accept if you want to become a profitable trader. The sooner you accept it, the sooner you can become profitable. What is essential to look for is a strategy with a positive statistical edge. This means that a strategy is a good one when the profitable trades are more frequent and/or gain more money than the losing trades.

On the whole, strategies are not set in stone. This means that individual investors must study them and apply them to their own personal objectives. Often, investors' personal strategy boils down to the level of risk tolerance and the aggressiveness by which they plan to implement their strategy. Based on these two concepts, investors can then develop their personal touch on their strategy.

So, sit back. We're going to be taking a good look at three simple strategies you can put into practice in the Forex market and start making profits.

Support and Resistance Strategy

Support and resistance levels can be used as indicators to trade Forex. From Chapter 2, you should be able to understand some basics of support and resistance points. Here are some tips to consider when you are observing the support and resistance levels.

- You should use the daily time frame or H4 in observing the trend because they indicate a more significant price level. The higher the time frame, the more significant the levels are;
- If you want to find a significant support and resistance

level, you must look for at least three points in the past where prices reacted to them.

In general, support and resistance levels allow us to buy near support (point 2 in fig. 3.1) and sell near resistance (points 1 and 3 in fig. 3.1).

When the candlestick closes well above a resistance level or well below a support level, it is a breakout signal (points 4 in fig. 3.1). A **breakout signal** is generally a strong indication that a substantial price movement is likely to happen. In this case, you should follow the possible new trend.

Figure 3.1: *Entry points for the support and resistance strategy (USD/JPY, h4 time frame) (Created with MT4. ©Metaquotes Software Corp.)*

In fig. 3.1, we see an example of the support and resistance strategy for a sideways market. We have several entry signals. For instance, we have a short signal highlighted on the 21st of August (point 1 at 106.69) and a long signal on the 28th of August (point 2 at 105.66). We also have another short signal on the 29th of August (point 3) and an entry signal on the 5th of September (point 4) after the breakout. Do not try entering a trade or breaking out before seeing the relevant signal, as highlighted in the graph. These signals are vital in ensuring that you stop making impulsive choices and base your trade on facts.

When do we exit the trade? The signal to exit should also be of great concern for any trader who wishes to succeed in the business. Since we buy above support and sell below resistance, you must first calculate any potential profits by considering an appropriate support and resistance level that prices can reach. When we enter a trade, to fix a profit target, we look for a significant price level that was touched (or crossed) in the past at least two or three times by prices moving in the same direction we are trading (long or short). In other words, we check how much prices can potentially move (the width of the possible movement).

For example, if we are in point 1 (fig. 3.2), we have a signal to open a short position (short selling). We see that prices in the past reached three times the price level of 105.65. That is our potential profit target. Then, we calculate the stop loss that is congruent with the risk we are taking (for instance, a risk to reward ratio of 1:2). This stop loss must fall outside the support or resistance channel that triggered our choice to enter the trade. If this is not the case, we should not enter the trade because our potential profit is too limited, and our stop loss is too close to current prices making the trade too risky.

If we enter a short trade on the 23rd of August at 106.45 (point 1) and the profit target is at 105.65, the potential price movement is 80 pips. If we choose to use a risk to reward ratio of 1:2, the risk should be 40 pips. This means that our stop-loss order should stand at 106.85. A close look at this value reveals that it is actually outside the support and resistance channel,

Figure 3.2: *Stop loss and profit target (USD/JPY, h4 time frame) (Created with MT4. ©Metaquotes Software Corp.)*

which is okay. The danger only occurs if this value falls within the support and resistance channel because there is a high probability that prices reach the stop loss during the trade.

Let's now see the example of a breakout for the USD/JPY pair. On the 5th of September, we have a breakout signal, as it is highlighted in figure 3.3 (point 1) and in figure 3.1 (point 4). These graphs represent the same pair but in different timeframes (daily and H4).

At the breakout, we open a long position on USD/JPY. When do we exit the trade? We have four different scenarios:

1. We get an opposite signal: if we get an opposite signal (the candlestick closes above/below the line), we exit the trade;

2. We reach the profit target. To set the profit target, we can use the method mentioned above: we look for a level in the graph touched or crossed at least two or three times in the past by prices moving in the same direction of the trade. In the example in fig 3.3, we buy at a

breakout signal (point 1); a possible profit target could be at 108.40 (+171 pips) because this width was already covered three times in the past (points A, B, and C). We can use a higher time frame (for example, a daily time frame) to help us out;

3. We set a trailing stop: if we are in profit, we can use a trailing stop to protect our gains;

4. We reach the stop-loss price. We should set the stop-loss order at a minimum of 20 pips below/above a significant top or bottom of prices. As soon as we are in good profit, we should move our stop loss at break-even.

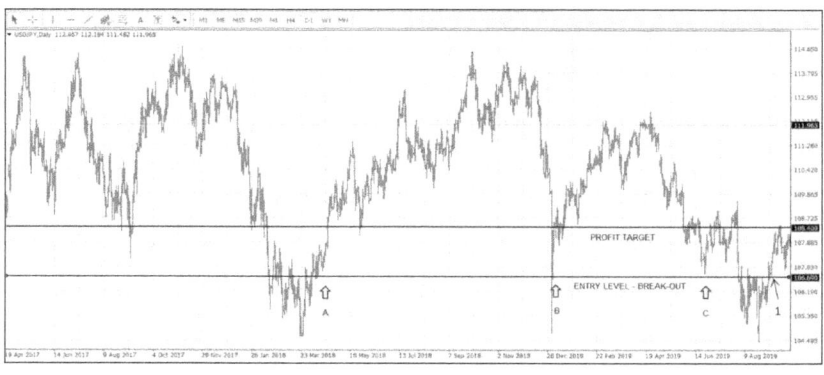

Figure 3.3: *Profit target for breakout strategy (USD/JPY, daily time frame) (Created with MT4. ©Metaquotes Software Corp.)*

Moving Average Strategy

The other strategy you can use to make profits in Forex is the moving average approach. We have established that you can use the moving average to spot the support and resistance points. Furthermore, you can use the MA crossovers to get entry and exit signals. In this strategy, we consider the 14, 20, and 50-periods MA.

The MA50 is used to give you an idea of the trend. If prices are above the MA50 it is a signal of an upward trend. If prices are below the MA50 it is a signal of a downward trend. It is advisable to trade in the direction of the trend using this kind of trading indicators. For instance, in the graph in fig. 3.4, the MA14 crosses the MA20 giving you an entry signal for a short selling. Your entry signal comes if you only consider crosses in the direction of the trend and if the cross's candlestick is the same sign as the trend. In any other case, the signal is not valid, and you have to wait until you spot a candlestick of the same sign of the trend before you make your move. In the

Figure 3.4: *Entry signal for the moving average strategy (USD/CAD, h4 time frame) (Created with MT4. ©Metaquotes Software Corp.)*

graph in fig. 3.4, the signal on the 10th of October provides the best scenario where the 14-periods MA crosses from above to below the 20-periods MA, giving a bearish signal. In this case, the candlestick was bullish, which means that we had to wait for the bearish candlestick, which provided the short entry signal. After that, you can see that the USD/CAD showed a substantial downward movement.

The exit signal should be in any instance where the opposite happens. You should also have your stop loss at least 20 pips above a significant high if you have a short position or below a significant low if you have a long position. In our example, the ideal stop loss should be at 1.3365, given that a significant high is at 1.3345 (see fig. 3.5).

Figure 3.5: *Stop loss for the moving average strategy (USD/CAD, h4 time frame) (Created with MT4. ©Metaquotes Software Corp.)*

Countertrend Strategy

You can also look out for countertrend signals if you want to use oscillators in making your trade decisions. About the Relative Strength Index, your entry signal comes when the indicator goes above 70 or below 30. In this case, we only wait for the indicator to move back into the 70-30 range, and we are ready to enter the trade (see fig. 3.6). For the RSI graph, we look at the daily or even weekly time frame. Oscillators' major problem is when prices are in trend because they can stay in the overbought or oversold area for a long time, giving you many false signals. Your job here is to look for a **divergence** to confirm a change in trend. Like in fig. 3.7, the indication is often double bottom or double top pattern with a higher top

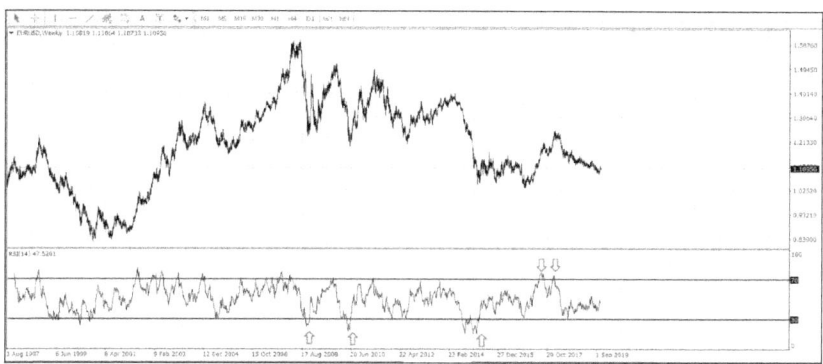

Figure 3.6: *Entry points for the countertrend strategy with RSI (EUR/USD, weekly time frame) (Created with MT4. ©Metaquotes Software Corp.)*

Figure 3.7: *Divergence with 14-periods RSI (EUR/USD, weekly time frame) (Created with MT4. ©Metaquotes Software Corp.)*

or a lower bottom not confirmed in the RSI. This is called a divergence between prices and RSI values.

Divergence is a strong indication of a change in price direction. The probabilities that this is going to happen are very high. The higher the time frame of analysis, the higher the chances are. At this stage, you determine that the momentum is about to shift and take the right action.

You may also opt for the stochastic approach in deciding

Figure 3.8: *Entry signal for the countertrend strategy with Stochastic (USD/CAD, h4 time frame) (Created with MT4. ©Metaquotes Software Corp.)*

entry and exit signals. We have already talked about the 80-20 range of the stochastic oscillator. If the indicator goes outside the 80-20 area, you have to wait until it is back inside the 80-20 area to make your entry move (see fig. 3.8). For the stochastic, you have to observe both the indicator and its average moving back into the 80–20 area. If the indicator moves into the 90-10 regions, you have even a stronger signal.

For the stochastic graph, you can use lower time frames than the H4, as is the case with RSI. However, lower time frames are also too noisy. This means that with a lower time frame, you have a chance of getting plenty of false signals. As for the RSI, *the signal gets stronger if we have a divergence.* To confirm the change in trend, look out for the double bottom or double top pattern.

We get an exit signal if the oscillators (RSI and Stochastic) reach the opposite side of the oversold or overbought area. Furthermore, we can set a stop loss of 20 pips below a significant

Figure 3.9: *Divergence with 20-periods Stochastic (USD/CAD, h4 time frame) (Created with MT4. ©Metaquotes Software Corp.)*

bottom or above a significant top.

How to Set the Stop Loss

The stop-loss order helps you limit your potential losses if a position you have chosen goes against your forecast. If you want to be successful in any trade, you must learn to use the stop-loss order, and you must make it a part of all your trades. First, it is important to note that every position you take should be out of conviction. You can use any of the above entry and exit strategies to determine the right time to enter a position and when it is time to exit. However, there are times when your predictions go wrong, even after considering all the crucial aspects discussed above. The stop-loss order can help you to fix most issues related to the wrong trade signal and to salvage your capital during your trading activity.

We will set the stop loss of at least 20 pips, which should be the case for most trades. If you position your stop loss 20 pips below or above a significant high or a significant low, you are guaranteed to save some amount if the trade goes against your prediction. This can be applied to any trade, whether you are buying or selling.

However, there is a risk factor to consider when using the stop-loss order, as it might cost you potential profits. In most cases, people rely on stop loss when they are not around to monitor the trade. Sometimes it can happen that your stop-loss is triggered, and just after that, prices start moving exactly in the direction you anticipated. In this case, you feel like the market makes fun of you. These are the experiences that will induce you not to use the stop loss. If you can manually follow up on the position, you can try to make individual considerations before implementing the stop-loss order. But it is not suitable for beginners because it requires a lot of experience and huge discipline.

Furthermore, statistics are in favor of the stop loss. Small and controlled losses are manageable and give you the opportunity to recoup back your money. If you don't use the stop loss, the chances are that a big loss will occur, and your account will be wiped out.

When setting up your stop-loss order, you should consider the risk-reward ratio too. As a matter of fact, this ratio should determine the number of pips you use when setting up the stop loss. In most cases, it is advisable to use a risk-reward ratio of 1:1.5 or 1:2. For example, if the potential gain is 100 pips, your stop loss should be 50 pips on the scale of 1:2, which is well within the recommended range.

Correct Position Sizing Formula

With all that said, the strategies indicated above can only lead, on average, to just a little more than a 50% chance of success. You should not bank all your money on a position just because the indicators are right or because the support and resistance points are encouraging. You may choose to combine one or two of the above strategies to increase your chances of success to 60% or 70%. Even in that case, you still have to invest sparingly.

You should choose the amount you invest in each position based on the risk factors involved. As you already know, the bigger the lot, the higher the risk. **My suggestion is to risk no more than 2% of your trading capital per each trade.** You can use the following formula to calculate the right position size before entering a trade.

Position size = (available capital $*$ % risk per trade)/(Stop loss in pips $*$ value per pips)

For example, if you run a USD account and want to trade the EUR/USD with an 80 pips stop-loss, you should determine the position size based on the following formula:

Total risk per trade 2%
Stop loss in pips = 80
Value per pip = $10
Available capital =$10,000
Position size = (10000 * 0.02)/(80 * 10) = 0.25 lots

This means that you have to invest 0.25 lots if you want to risk a maximum of $200 per trade (2% in a $10,000 account).

Diversification

In investment circles, you often hear the term "diversify." However, it's not always clear what this term is alluding to. In many cases, diversifying investments is more about spreading the wealth, so to speak, rather than allocating more funds into a specific market. When you diversify, what you are essentially doing is spreading out your investments and distributing them among various asset classes. This is important, particularly if you are already invested in stocks.

It's essential to consider this proposition, as investing in tech, agricultural, and mining stocks is not diversification. Yes, they are various industries, but they are still the same asset class. Generally speaking, if the market drops, they all drop even if they belong to different sectors. In this regard, it's like putting all "your eggs in one basket." It might seem like they are different baskets, but it's still the same basket in reality.

Proper diversification occurs when you allocate your investment dollars into various asset classes. This implies investing in precious metals, commodities, currencies, stocks, and even hard assets such as real estate or private equities. Furthermore, it is wise to diversify also the portfolio invested in every single asset class. So, for example, if you have investments in stocks, diversify with more than one stock; if you have investments in currencies, diversify with more than one currency; if you have assets in real estate, diversify in different units in different locations, and so on.

When you diversify, you can hedge risk. This means that if one asset class declines, for whatever reason, you stand to make up the difference with another asset class. In the worst of cases, the profits from one asset class offset the losses of another. In the best of circumstances, all asset classes make money for your portfolio. In the end, you reduce the overall risk of being wiped out by a so-called "black swan" event.

The key to diversification is to invest in uncorrelated assets. This means the assets themselves don't hold any influence over each other. This is a vital part of adequate diversification.

For Forex investors, those predominantly investing in Forex and not just dabbling in the currency market, diversification has implied branching out into other asset classes. Nevertheless, it's important to note that diversifying for the sake of diversifying will not get you the results you are looking for. In this regard, it's all about diversifying into the right assets that will get you the results you are looking to achieve.

Consider this example:
Let's assume that you wish to invest in gold as a means of diversifying your portfolio. At the same time, you take a position in a pair such as AUD/USD. On the surface, it appears that you have diversified as gold (a precious metal) is a different asset class. However, Australia happens to be a leading producer of gold. The AUD depends on the gold price, given that Australia supplies gold to the world market. So, the changes in the price of gold affect the Australian economy, which then affects the currency's valuation.

As you can see from this example, gold and the AUD don't appear to be correlated on the surface. But when you dig deeper, they are. Therefore, proper diversification isn't about putting all of your eggs into one basket; it's about putting your eggs into the right basket. Consequently, when you are able to allocate your investments correctly, then you can maximize your return.

Diversification works when you are able to balance out the risk-reward equation. For instance, you might be able to make a great return on a single deal. As such, you might be tempted to go all-in. However, if something goes wrong, you may end up going broke on the deal.

By the same token, if you spread your investments out too far, then you might find that your returns will be far less than expected. This will end up leaving you disappointed with the performance of your portfolio. Consequently, it's best to find the right balance between risk and reward. Ultimately, in Forex trading, it's not so much about allocating your funds in a single trade or finding the largest number of trades. The idea is about allocating your funds in the best possible number of trades. Typically, this works out with roughly **three to four different, uncorrelated pairs at the same time.**

Correlation Strategy

When trading in various currency pairs, it's important to keep an eye on the pairs you are trading. On the surface, it might appear that you are trading in a diversified range of pairs. However, it could very well be that you are trading with currency pairs that are correlated. Correlation occurs when you have two pairs that deal with the same currency. You might think that as they are two different currency pairs (even if with one common currency), they are different trades. Superficially, that would appear to be the case. When you dig deeper, though, you will find that placing multiple trades involving a common currency is like placing the same trade several times.

Let's look at this example: You have decided to place two trades, one using the AUD/USD pair and the other using the EUR/USD pair. At first sight, these trades seem uncorrelated as the market forces between all currencies involved are different.

Upon closer inspection, you'll find that these pairs are correlated as they have the US Dollar in common. So, even if the dynamics among all three currencies may be completely different, any shifts in the US Dollar value will affect both currency pairs. The changes in, say, the AUD/USD pair may end up affecting your performance on the EUR/USD.

To get over this, a good rule of thumb to keep in mind is to avoid having multiple positions open in which you have currencies in common. As such, if you have a EUR/USD position, you could complement that with an AUD/NZD position. Both of these trades lack a common currency, thereby reducing the amount of risk involved.

Now, if you were to place multiple trades with a currency in common, it's always a good idea to split the risk. Generally speaking, my suggestion is to risk less than 2% on each trade. Consequently, in the EUR/USD and AUD/USD positions, you should split the risk and risk no more than 1% for each pair. That way, if your idea of the market is wrong, you are risking no more than 2% total.

Golden Rules of Money Management

While Forex can provide you with attractive returns without the hassle that comes with trading stocks, the fact of the matter is that it requires you to develop a structured approach. This approach will enable you to avoid many of the pitfalls that the average investor generally runs into. When you stick to the "Golden Rules of Money Management," you will find that being successful is a lot easier than you could have ever thought about.

Warren Buffet summed these rules up best by saying, "Rule no.1: Never lose money. Rule no.2: Never forget rule no.1".

This statement might seem rather simplistic, but the fact is that it is the most effective way to manage your money. If you are keen on not losing money, you will be cognizant of making the best possible deal every time.

As such, money management refers to a set of rules that are related to the management of invested capital in trading. This means that you ought to have a clear understanding of the rules you are utilizing when playing the markets. Failure to observe these rules may lead you to sustain significant losses. Money management can be broken down into two rules. The first is risk management, and the second is position sizing.

Risk management boils down to risk aversion or risk tolerance. All investors have a personal level of risk aversion or tolerance. Some investors are more inclined to risk aversion, that is, avoiding risk as much as possible. Other investors may be more inclined to risk tolerance that is taking on a higher degree of risk. Although, it should be said that "the greater the risk, the greater the reward."

Beyond the obvious assertion referring to the lack of certainty in a trade, the risk is correlated to position sizing. Position sizing refers to the amount of your investment capital you are willing to allocate for a particular trade. This means that the higher the position size, the greater the risk.

Consider this situation.
A single trade that involves 100% of your investment capital would involve the highest possible amount of risk. This is due to the fact that if the trade doesn't work out, you could end up completely wiped out.

On the other hand, if you invest 0% of your capital (that is, you don't make a trade), you have the lowest possible risk as you don't expose yourself to the market. As such, the size of your position determines the amount of risk you are taking on.

Based on this premise, money management's main goal is to avoid losing your entire investment capital in a small number of trades. Hence, making sure that you avoid sinking too much of your investment capital into individual trades ought to be your primary focus. That way, if a trade goes down the drain, you would not risk losing a significant part of your portfolio.

One of the most important concepts regarding money management is making up your losses. Novice investors tend to get caught up in "doubling down "on their losses. For instance, if you place a $100 trade and lose your entire capital, you might be tempted to place a $200 trade to make your money back.

This type of trading is not only foolish but a ticking time bomb. You never know when the bomb will go off, leaving you wiped out completely. Table 3.1 shows the percentage of profit you would need to gain based on the percentage of your losses in order to break-even.

As you can see, the greater the amount you lose, the greater the profit would have to be just to recoup your losses. So, if you placed 95% of your capital and lost, you would have to make a profit of 1900% just to get back to where you started. Needless to say, this is unrealistic.

On the other hand, if you lost 5% of your investment capital, you would need to make 5.26% to get back to where you started. Additionally, a 50% loss means you would have to double your winning just to make your money back. This type of expectation is unsustainable as there is no way you can double your money back every time. Even if it doesn't sound like the most exciting strategy, but erring on the side of caution is the best way for you to ensure that your trading account won't be wiped out in a few trades. This is why it's crucial

Initial Capital	%Loss	$ Loss	Account Balance	% Gain Needed to Break Even
$10,000	-5.00%	$500	$9,500	5.26%
$10,000	-10.00%	$1,000	$9,000	1.11%
$10,000	-20.00%	$2,000	$8,000	25.00%
$10,000	-30.00%	$3,000	$7,000	42.86%
$10,000	-40.00%	$4,000	$6,000	66.67%
$10,000	-50.00%	$5,000	$5,000	100.00%
$10,000	-60.00%	$6,000	$4,000	150.00%
$10,000	-70.00%	$7,000	$3,000	233.33%
$10,000	-80.00%	$8,000	$2,000	400.00%
$10,000	-90.00%	$9,000	$1,000	900.00%
$10,000	-95.00%	$9,500	$500	1900.00%

Table 3.1: % Gain needed to break-even compared to losses

to consider the need to limit your position size to manageable levels. That way, getting back into the black won't be nearly as difficult.

With that in mind, let's take a closer look at the golden rules of money management, which will help you become a successful investor by hedging risk much more effectively.

- The maximum amount of investment capital that you ought to risk in a single trade should not exceed 2%. While you could potentially invest your entire capital in the market, each individual trade should not exceed 2%. That way, if you were wiped out in a single trade, you could never lose more than 2%. So, a modest return on future trades could easily make up the difference.
- Use your stop loss in pips and your risk percentage to set up your trade's right position size. Calculate correctly your position in relation to the type of trade

and investment capital you are risking, choosing the right amount of mini or micro lots to use for each trade.

- Take diversification and correlation into account when placing your positions. If you choose to go with two positions that are correlated, open up each one at the same time. Also, apply the 2% rule meaning that both positions combined should not exceed the 2% threshold. Essentially, this would spread out the risk at 1% for each position.

- Always set up your stop-loss. Make sure that you never cancel it no matter what. It could save you if things went bad in a hurry. In addition, always take the profit no matter what.

- Make sure to get the risk-reward ratio right. This will help your trading to have a positive statistical edge. Choose trades with a risk to reward ratio of at least 1:1.5, better 1:2, or even higher. That way, you will always land your trades in the range you are looking for.

- Never forget to set up a bearable drawdown. A drawdown refers to how much your trading account is down from the peak. Setting up a maximum drawdown in your account will save your remaining capital. Please bear in mind that if you lose your entire capital, it's game over. I suggest you consider a maximum drawdown of 8%–10% as the total loss of your trading account. This can be easily reached, for example, with four or five stop-losses in a row. When this drawdown value is reached, your trading should be automatically halted. Use this stoppage to assess your strategy and look for any mistakes you might be making. Then, make sure you take corrective actions so that you can avoid any future mistakes.

- The amount of money you choose to invest in trading

depends on the amount of capital you have available. Naturally, it's not wise to invest your life savings. This would be foolish as you would be risking your family's livelihood. Nevertheless, it's a subjective matter. So, common sense should reign supreme here. Make sure that whatever amount of money you choose to invest will not undermine your loved ones' quality of life. If anything, it should be an amount of money that would not damage your finances in a significant manner if it were completely lost.

- Also, don't reinvest all of your profits. Always keep a portion for yourself. This could be put aside for saving or perhaps could go toward paying off something important, such as debt. Please remember that it's good to use some of your winning for nice things such as taking a trip or buying something useful. So, try to avoid the nagging feeling of having to reinvest all of your winnings. This way, you can avoid becoming too much cocky and self-confident in your trading and start risking more than what you should do.

With these golden rules, you will come out ahead most of the time. While there are no guarantees in any market, you can be sure that you will have a good chance to come out ahead every time. So, take the time to go over these rules again and again until they become second nature to you.

Backtesting Strategies

One of the biggest sins that investors make is basing their investment decisions on scarce, unreliable, or incomplete data and information. This way, the chances of being successful come down to luck. They think or feel an investment or trading strategy is a good one, but they don't have any proof of it.

Backtesting is one of the most efficient means that investors have to determine if their strategies are truly effective or not. In short, backtesting consists of pressure testing a strategy, with the use of historical data, to determine if the strategy was truly effective in the past. You need to find out if the strategy you want to follow has a positive statistical edge. This means you have to determine if the strategy will give you a profit in the long run.

To backtest a strategy, it is a good idea to get various data samples. The farther back you can go, the better. Often, two or three years of data are a good place to start. Anything less than that might make it tough for you to really see the patterns you are looking to spot. This is especially true if you spot a pattern that has recently taken place. As such, you need to go as far back as you can to see if this movement has happened before.

Most investors feel comfortable working with ten years' worth of historical data. There are several reasons why going that far back makes sense. Since currency is tied to several macro and microeconomic factors, more extended data sets make a lot more sense as they are able to smooth out singularities in data. For example, a nation's economy may have an unexpected shock due to a natural disaster such as a hurricane. So, under the optics of that particular event, that nation's economy might look weak. However, under the broader scope of ten years, it can be easier to spot reliable trends.

Historical data can also take into account worldwide phenomena such as recessions, external shocks, and historical events of international magnitude such as wars and migration. All of these elements can be reflected in the data. As such, you can determine trends and overall shifts in currency valuation.

Lastly, a more extended set of data can provide you with an understanding of a currency's dynamics. For instance, if a country underwent fiscal reform, you would be able to spot the effects of such reform. However, if the reform has been rather recent, the data you would be working with may not accurately reflect such reforms' full effects. Therefore, having a broader sample would give you a much more in-depth picture of the situation surrounding any given currency dynamics.

On the whole, backtest a strategy as much as you can. That will give you the peace of mind that your assumptions are correct. Moreover, you want to make sure that your calculations make sense within the scope of the historical data that is available to you.

Here are two ways in which you can backtest any strategy:

- **Automated backtesting:** Most solid trading platforms contain trading algorithms that enable you to backtest any strategy. So, all you need to do is set your trade, select the data set that you wish to use, for example, a period comprising 2010 to 2020, and then run the simulation. The software does everything for you. In some cases, you may have to purchase an additional module. Once you get the results from your backtesting simulation, you can study them to determine if you feel they are accurate. A careful study of the results would enable you to make good sense of them.

- **Manual Backtesting:** If you choose to conduct a manual backtest, you must go back to the charts containing the historical information you are looking to utilize and examine, bar by bar, how the strategy would have played out. This way of backtesting does not require any additional software. You also have the advantage of being able to run through data with a fine-tooth comb. The main disadvantage is that it is enormously time-consuming.

Here are four steps that you can follow to backtest strategies manually:

- First, pick a currency pair. Then, enter a date parameter in the data you are looking to sample. Then, apply any other tools you want to incorporate into the sample. For instance, you can look at the moving average to determine a moving average crossover.
- Next, scroll through the chart by sifting through the sample bar by bar. Each bar might indicate potential trade setups that you can use.
- After that, look at the points in which potential trade setups have occurred. You can track their results through the use of a simple spreadsheet. In this spreadsheet, enter the following data: date, point of entry, stop-loss point, take-profit, and risk to reward ratio. If there is any other relevant information, you want to add, be sure that it includes such data, as well.
- Lastly, repeat this process with any other potential trade setups. This will enable you to test the effectiveness of your strategy. You can determine it to be effective by seeing if the patterns repeat themselves. If you find that the results are consistent, you may very well have a good strategy to put into practice on the live platform.

While manual backtesting may sound time-consuming, it's certainly worth the time and effort as you can be completely sure that your model is accurate and worth running on the live platform.

Please be sure to backtest your assumptions with various

timeframes. Sometimes, a strategy works with a higher time-frame but not with a lower timeframe and vice versa. In doing this, you can determine if there is a reasonable possibility that your assumptions will work out. Again, charts can be deceiving. So, it's best to do your due diligence.

As I already mentioned before in this book, strategies derived from the technical analysis have, on average, just a 50% chance of success. So, if you test them singularly, you are likely not going to have any positive results. If you combine them, your chances can increase, but also the difficulties to backtest can increase. For instance, backtesting the support and resistance strategy can be tricky because it is quite subjective how you determine relevant points in the graph. Experience can change the outcome. The human factor is very difficult to be systemized and backtested in traditional ways. Every person will obtain different results, even starting from the same strategies and information. Furthermore, keep in mind that if a strategy had positive results in the past, it is not a guarantee that it will have the same in the future. And vice versa.

My suggestion is to use also your results as backtesting. Choose your strategy and start with paper trading. After a while, check your performance and look if you make some mistakes not following the strategy correctly. Adjust your trading and start the test again. When you get consistent results, start trading with a small capital and with a high risk-reward ratio (let's say 1:2.5 or 1:3). As you trade, check your percentage of success. If you go over 50%, you can decrease this ratio until 1:1.5 or 1:2. After a reasonable amount of time (let's say at least six months), recheck your strategy and results, the mistakes you made, and the strategy's potential performance. This is what I call "tailor-made backtesting ".

At the end of the day, making money with a strategy is all about testing it to see if your assumptions, for any given currency pair, hold up under closer scrutiny. As we have mentioned throughout this book, taking the time to do your due diligence on your trades is a vital factor in making as much as you can in Forex trading. Those investors who are unwilling to spend time and effort into research will find that they don't make nearly as much money as they would have hoped. By putting in the work that is needed to set up your trades, you can be sure that you will make more and more money as your skills and experience help you achieve greater proficiency.

Choose your Own Trading Style

One of the great things that come with trading the Forex market is that you get a lot of options. You can choose the pairs that you want to invest in. You can choose how much money you want to invest. You can choose the amount of risk that you are willing to take with each trade. And you can even choose the strategy that you want to go with. The amount of return you will get will be based on the options that you choose, how much you spend, and how the trade goes. You have to make another choice, and that will affect your results enormously: your trading style. There are different trading styles that you can choose from. Some of the most common ones are:

Position trading

The first option that you can choose is position trading. This is going to be a long-term trading practice, which can range from a few months on to a few years. Many people who work with the Forex market to supplement their income or to save up for their retirement choose position trading. This trading style can allow the trader to have some more time to watch the trends that go on in the market before making any decisions to buy or sell a currency pair.

This style will be skewed towards being an investment option, but you can utilize both the short-term and long-term strategies to make them work. If you are a position trader, you are more like an investor than a trader. Position traders will spend their time looking at both the weekly and the monthly charts. But unlike some of the other styles that we will discuss, they will not worry so much about the small daily fluctuations in prices. They are more worried about the trend and how that is going to affect their investment.

Day Trading

The next strategy that you can consider working with is going to be called day trading. When working in this trading style, you will enter into a new trade or purchase an asset and then sell that same asset on the same day. A day trader is never going to hold onto their positions overnight. You need to make sure that the trade is completed before the market closes.

A day trader should take a lot of time looking at charts and working on technical analysis in order to figure out any of the trends that come along. You need to get a lot of information to pick out the currency pairs that can make you some good money in a short amount of time.

Day trading includes several small trades over the day. You will not be able to make a huge amount of money on each of them. But when you do well with the majority of these trades, those small and frequent profits can add up and lead to some good profits over time. This kind of trading is good if you are looking to replace your income because you can make some good money, and you need a lot of time to monitor your trades during the day.

Swing Trading

For some beginners, day trading can be a little complicated to work with, and they may not like all of the fast-paced action that occurs in this kind of trading. But probably they still want the chance to trade Forex and see the same profits. This is where swing trading can come into play.

With swing trading, you will hold onto the trade from anywhere between one day to two weeks. It is similar to day trading in the sense that you will spend your time looking at graphs to look for short-term fluctuations of prices to get some profits out of them.

With swing trading, as with day trading, you won't worry so much about fundamental analysis. You won't be in the trade for a long time, so the fundamentals don't really matter all that much, except for some particular news that can impact the market. Swing trading is a great option to choose from, and it is my favorite. I mostly trade in this way. My trades last between two and ten days on average.

How to Choose Your Own Trading Style

Now that we have talked about a few of the options that you can use, it is time to pick out your own trading style. Picking out a good trading style can be hard, but you first need to make sure that you know what you would like to get out of the Forex trading.

There are a few factors that you can consider, including:

- The size of your account: The more money you have to get started, the more options you have.

- How much time you will be able to devote yourself to your trades: If you can only spend a bit of time each day on trading, then day trading is not the best option for you.
- Your experience level when it comes to trading: Beginners should pick a strategy that involves less risk and less work so that they can learn more about the market before moving into some of the styles that take more work. Swing trading or position trading (investing) are the best options for beginners.
- Your risk tolerance: Some people just aren't able to tolerate any kind of risk at all. They will stick with some relatively low-risk options and be happy with the returns that they can get. They don't like big swings in their portfolio's value, or they don't like to go to bed knowing they have open positions in the market.
- Your own personality: You also need to take the time to understand your own personality and how it will affect your trading. How much can you handle stress? Can you manage your emotions? Are you disciplined?

For the most part, the amount of time you would like to spend on trading will be the most relevant in picking up the trading style you would like to go with. For example, if you have a busy schedule and can only give a few hours each week to monitor your charts, you will probably want to be a position trader.

On the other hand, if you can spend a lot of time looking over the charts and picking the right options for you, you can try swing or day trading. Over time, you may even want to diversify your portfolio and find that having more than one of these investment styles can bring in the most money.

4 Main Strategies in Detail

When investing in Forex, having go-to strategies that you can put into practice, day after day, make all the difference between making money and missing out on profits. That's why it's important to dig deeper into strategies that you can feel comfortable using as part of your daily trading plan.

For these strategies to make sense in your everyday trading efforts, it's important to keep a close eye on the indicators that are a part of your technical analysis endeavors. As we have stated at various points throughout this book, doing your research will pay off in the long run. Please bear in mind that the more time and effort you put into studying your strategies, the better the results will be.

The strategies that we are going to be discussing in this chapter are the ones we saw in Chapter 3, but we will study them in detail. They are some go-to strategies that you can keep in your playbook. Deploy them at any time, though do make sure that you have done your due diligence.

So, without further ado, let's get down to each one of the strategies to look at them step-by-step with examples in real trading.

Support and Resistance Strategy Step-by-Step

When looking at this strategy, it's important to keep in mind the market's overall trend. We will use a daily or H4 timeframe. At least six months of data should provide you with an accurate picture of the trend in the currency pairing of your choice.

In this example, we are going to be taking a look at the GBP/JPY pair in the daily timeframe. In figure 4.1, you will find a downward or bearish trend, as identified by the trend line. This is where our focus will lie. Also, please note that this data set ranges for about roughly a year. As such, there is abundant data that can be used to plot support and resistance points. Now, let's take a look at how you can use the previous chart to set up your trade.

Figure 4.1: *GBP/JPY trend (Dataset: from January 2019 to April 2020, daily time frame) (Created with MT4. ©Metaquotes Software Corp.)*

Step #1: Determine the trend

Using the chart as a reference, we can infer that the outlook on the chart, at least for the foreseeable future, is bearish. So, we will look for a bearish trade. This trend can be identified at plain sight by looking at the movement in the chart itself. However, the plotting of the trend line makes it abundantly clear where the trend lies. Based on this trend line, we can determine a bearish outlook for the short to medium-term. Given that there is a clear trend in this market, it's better to make a trade trend following than going countertrend. We decide to short sell the GBP/JPY pair, opening a short position.

While there is the possibility of a reversal, it's better to follow trends as this would give you the best chances of making a profit. Unless you have reason to believe that the trend will reverse, it's best to go with the flow. This is true unless the price crosses over the trend line. If that happens, we wait to see if the candlestick closes well over it. In that case, it is a signal that the mid-term trend is going to change. Remember that the more points a trend line touches in the graphs, the more significant the trend line is. Two points are the minimum to draw a trend line. If the points are three or more, it is even better.

Step #2: Find an entry point

It's important to look at the various resistance and support levels to determine the entry point. In this example, we can find that 130.59 was hit three times over the span of analysis. This indicates that it would serve as a good entry point. This level is highlighted by the 1, 2, and 3 points in the chart in figure 4.1. As such, you need to keep an eye on this level. For instance, if you see the candlestick closing below this price, 130.59, then you have an entry signal as you are poised to see a breakout.

Figure 4.2: *GBP/JPY trend (Dataset: from September 2013 to April 2020, weekly time frame) (Created with MT4. ©Metaquotes Software Corp.)*

Step #3: Find an exit point

Just as important as the entry point is the exit point. Like before, we need to take a look at the various support and resistance levels in the chart. A clear support level has been spotted at 126.88, 371 pips downwards (see profit target in figure 4.1). As such, we have identified a potential exit point for this particular trade.

Step #4: Review entry and exit points at a higher time frame

To validate the setup, we need to look at the same support and resistance levels at a higher time frame. In this case, we can see in figure 4.2 the same data in a weekly timeframe. This is done to determine if the support and resistance levels touch more points in the past prices so that they are more reliable (and the probability prices will react to them are higher).

Step #5: Deciding whether to enter the trade

Let's take a closer look at the potential entry point. We are considering a possible entry price at 129.30 and an exit one at 126.88. This means that we assume that the candlestick closes below 130.59 and that we have a potential entry at 129.30. To decide if we enter the trade, we have to check if our stop loss will fall outside the channel we draw with the support and resistance levels. It is now important to consider our risk-to-reward ratio, for example, 1:2 for this particular case. This ratio would then allow us to calculate our stop-loss. In this case, the stop-loss price would be at 130.51.

Let's see how we get this number. We can calculate this by taking the support level at 126.88 as the profit target (as it has been touched multiple times throughout the time range analyzed). So, 129.30 (−) 126.88 would give us a result of 2.42. Under this assumption, we would be potentially making 242 pips of potential profit. Since we are assuming a 1:2 risk-to-reward ratio, this would work out to 242 / 2 = 121. This indicates that we would have 121 pips of a potential loss. So, to determine the stop-loss point, we would add 129.30 and 121, which equals 130.51. This is the possible stop–loss price to consider as part of this trade.

Based on these results, we **would not enter the trade** as the stop-loss point of 130.51 is within the channel we have drawn. As such, it's better to look for a better entry point.

Let's now assume that the potential entry price is 129.80, not 129.30. In this case, maintaining the same risk–to –reward ratio, we would have the stop–loss level at 131.26. Let's see why. We have 129.80 (−) 126.88 = 2.92, or 292 pips of potential profit. By the same token, 292 / 2 = 146 pips of a potential loss. This works out to the following stop–loss price: 129.80 (+) 1.46 = 131.26.

In this case, **we would enter the trade** as the stop-loss is outside the channel we are analyzing. It's also important to double-check to see if the stop-loss is at least 20 pips outside of the channel. If so, then you can go ahead and confirm the trade.

Step #6: Defining your position sizing

Please do this according to the guidelines and formula explained in Chapter 3.

Step #7: Ending the trade

Close the trade at the profit target or if you have a reliable signal of a potential reversal in the trend or that the breakout was a false signal. Furthermore, if your position goes in good profit (let's say 50% of the potential profit), you can move your stop loss to break even.

Moving Average Strategy Step-by-Step

In investing, the moving average is perhaps the most important indicator you can use to determine trends. It's important to keep a close eye on moving averages as they will tell you where the price action looks to move at any given point. In this strategy, we are going to take a closer look at the moving average of the AUD/USD pair for a period of roughly ten months (see fig. 4.3). We'll be focusing on a specific part of the chart, which highlights the overall trend up to now.

Step #1: Look at the chart to determine the trend

First off, we will look at the chart plotted for the period in question. This will help us to determine if there is a trend. In the chart in figure 4.3, we plotted the 14, 20, and 50-periods moving average in the daily timeframe. As you can see, prices are well above the 50-period moving average. This is a clear

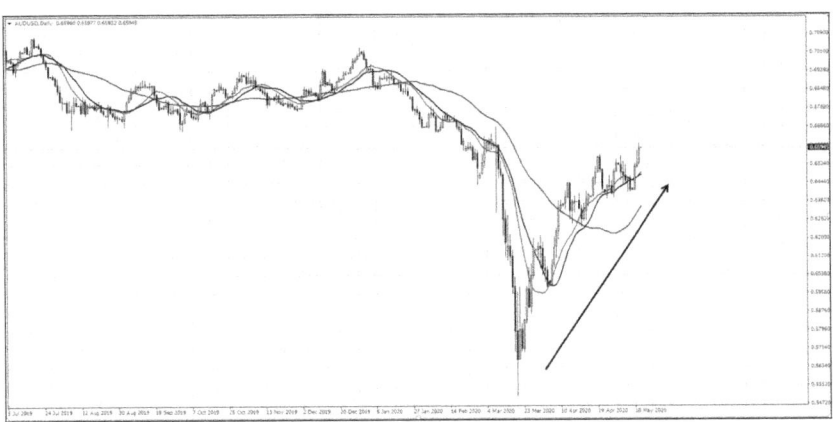

Figure 4.3: AUD/USD trend (Dataset: from July 2019 to May 2020, daily time frame) (Created with MT4. ©Metaquotes Software Corp.)

signal of a bullish trend. As such, it is safe to assume that the overall outlook for the medium-term is bullish.

Step #2: Look for the crossover

When trading with moving averages, it is important to spot points where there is a crossover among the different moving averages. When you spot a crossover, it's possible to determine an entry point. In this case, we can look at the 14-period and 20-period moving average in a lower timeframe, such as H4 (see figure 4.4). At the point where you can spot a crossover, you have a potential entry point. This implies that you can get in when the prices move down so that you can catch the upswing.

For this particular chart, we have taken the H4 timeframe, although you could even look at an hourly chart. Please bear in mind that the more timeframes you can compare, the easier it will be to determine the validity of your entry and exit points. For the sake of this exercise, we will assume an entry price of

Figure 4.4: *Trade setup using the moving average strategy (AUD/USD, H4 time frame) (Created with MT4. ©Metaquotes Software Corp.)*

0.6486, as this is the close signaled by the candlestick (figure 4.4).

Step #3: Confirm the trend

When looking to determine your entry point's validity, it is important to double-check to see if the sign of the candlestick (bullish or bearish) indicates the same signal as that of the moving averages' crossing (and consequently of the trend). If this is the case, as in figure 4.4, then you have a valid entry point. If not, it would be wise to wait for this signal that will confirm your entry point.

Step #4: Setup your stop-loss and take profit

Generally speaking, your stop-loss should be 20 pips above a significant top (in the case of a short trade) or 20 pips below a significant bottom (in the case of a long trade). This is a good rule of thumb to keep in mind when entering a trade using moving averages. For this particular example, the significant bottom is spotted at 0.6401 on May 15th (see figure 4.4). As such, if we subtract 20 pips, we get a result of 0.6381 (0.6401 (-) 0.002 = 0.6381). Under this assumption, we have a stop-loss of 105 pips, considering an entry price of 0.6486, as said before.

Another important rule to keep in mind is that your take profit should be at least 1.5 to 2 times your potential stop-loss. In other words, this is your risk-to-reward ratio. For the sake of this exercise, we are going to use a risk-to-reward ratio of 1:1.5. Under the previous assumptions, the take profit would be +158 pips. This sets the profit price at 0.6644.

Next, go back into the data set to see if this price has been hit before while prices were moving in the same direction. In other words, check if prices covered the same width in the past. *If not, do not enter the trade.*

Furthermore, run the data sampling at various timeframes, that is, with higher and lower frequencies. At this point, it's worth looking to see how many times the price point was hit. If there is a recurrent pattern, then it is feasible for the trade to work out as it has already happened at some point in the past. This is pretty much the same as the "support and resistance"strategy. When you cannot spot the price being hit in the past, then the likelihood of the trade happening is much lower than you might expect, so do not enter the trade.

Step #5: Defining your position sizing

Please do this according to the guidelines and formula explained in Chapter 3.

Step #6: Closing the trade

Close the trade at the profit target or when you spot an opposite crossing signal. If you see a candlestick closing of the same sign at the crossover point, it is a signal of a potential reversal. Then go ahead and close your position. The longer you hold your position, the greater the likelihood of your profit to be reduced. Lastly, if your position goes in good profit (let's say 50% of the potential profit), you can move your stop loss to break even.

Countertrend Strategy Step-by-Step

With this strategy, you will open trades in the opposite direction of the trend. This is the opposite of what we have discussed in previous strategies that follow the trend. As such, you can play the countertrend to your advantage. However, you need to be aware of the signals that will indicate if such a strategy is feasible or not.

The step-by-step process discussed herein is similar for both the Relative Strength Index (RSI) and the Stochastic strategy. For the sake of this example, we are going to be following the RSI strategy. As for the Stochastic strategy, you would have to follow a similar step-by-step procedure.

Step #1: Check for overbought or oversold areas

The use of the RSI enables you to determine areas of potential overselling or overbuying. As such, run a sampling of data in a daily timeframe or even higher. This will allow you to see where these areas can be located. It is important to use a very high timeframe as using lower timeframes gives off a considerable number of false signals. The higher the frequency of the timeframe, the more these areas are reliable.

The chart in figure 4.5 provides a good example of these areas for the AUD/NZD currency pair. As you can see, there is a daily timeframe sampling of the data. We can identify an overbought area, as evidenced by a level of about 70. The

Figure 4.5: *Plotting the RSI in the graph (AUD/USD, daily time frame) (Created with MT4. ©Metaquotes Software Corp.)*

highlighted areas show the increase in the movements of the currency pair.

It should be noted that this is the only strategy that does not use the trend as its primary discretionary criteria. Consequently, when you use this strategy, you'll be moving countertrend most of the time. While it is possible to engage this strategy following the trend, it is far more likely to enter the trade at countertrend. So, don't be surprised to find yourself in this position most of the time.

Step #2: Check for divergence

Next, we are going to check to see if there is any divergence between the RSI and the actual prices. In the chart in figure 4.6, we can spot a divergence. When looking at prices, we can see increasing tops. When looking at the RSI, we can see decreasing tops.

As such, this price movement indicates a divergence. Now, given the fact that we can spot three tops in a row, which

Figure 4.6: *Divergence between RSI and prices (AUD/USD, daily time frame) (Created with MT4. ©Metaquotes Software Corp.)*

are correlated to the divergence, it is even a stronger signal for the expected price action. While it doesn't mean that the currency pair in question will actually drop, it does show a high degree of probability that it will happen.

Step #3: Observe the RSI movement

In this step, we are going to wait for the RSI to settle back into the range of 70 –30 before opening a short position. It's important to keep a close watch as this movement will eventually mark the specific point in which the entry point will emerge. Once we get the entry signal, we can move in. As you see in figure 4.7, a bear signal is observed on May 19. As such, we are going to assume an entry point at 1.7055.

Step #4: Setup a stop-loss and a take profit

As we have indicated previously, take 20 pips to set up your stop-loss point. In this case, we are going to take at least 20 pips above a significant top. In this example, we will take the top observed on May 18. The stop-loss is set at 1.0846

Figure 4.7: *Trade set-up using the RSI Strategy (AUD/USD, daily time frame) (Created with MT4. ©Metaquotes Software Corp.)*

(as you can see in figure 4.7). Ultimately, the stop-loss for this example is set at 91 pips in total. In order to set up the take-profit point, we need to consider 1.5 to 2 times the possible stop-loss. As such, this becomes our risk-to-reward ratio. For this example, we will assume a risk-to-reward ratio of 1:2. So, this puts the take-profit at +182 pips (91 * 2 = 182). Consequently, this puts the take profit at 1.0573.

To ensure your trade's effectiveness, check to see if there is any sign of the potential profit being hit in the data sampling. If the potential profit has been covered in the past, you can reasonably think it can happen again. If there is a history of recurrence, then the likelihood will be even greater. As such, you can be relatively sure that the profit will occur as there is a clear indication that it has happened before. In essence, this is the same approach as we have used in the previous two strategies.

Also, please go as far back as you can, using higher and lower timeframes, to double-check the occurrence of the price action. This ought to confirm if you are on the right track. Please keep in mind that the farther back you go, the better you can ascertain the effectiveness of your strategy.

Step #5: Defining your position sizing

Please do this according to the guidelines and formula explained in Chapter 3.

Step #6: Closing the trade

Close the trade at the profit target or when you get an indication of a reversal as shown by an opposite signal. As seen in figure 4.77, if you spot that the RSI has moved into the oversold area, then it is time to close the trade. Lastly, if your position goes in good profit (for example, 50% of the potential profit), you can move your stop loss to break even.

With the three strategies that we have outlined in this chapter, I am taking you by hand to your first trade done properly. Of course, nothing is guaranteed when it comes to investing. But with the use of these strategies in the manner that we have outlined them, you have a good chance at being successful.

5 Historical Background

The world's current monetary system is no accident. In fact, it has been the result of a number of phenomena that, at one point or another, affected the entire world. The progression to the monetary system that we know today has been a bumpy one, to say the least. In this chapter, we will examine the route the world's current monetary system has taken. In particular, we're going to be focusing on the events which occurred at the end of the 19th century and early 20th century. These events shaped the monetary system that reigned for much of the 20th century leading up to the evens of the 1970s, which ushered in the system we know today.

The Gold Standard

Monetary historians and economists are familiar with the "gold standard." This is a system that emerged in the latter half of the 19th century in Europe. The reasoning behind the gold standard was the need to have some type of physical backing to fiat currency. In this regard, virtually every country in the world fixed its currency to some weight of gold. As such, the valuation of a country's currency was expressed through its value in gold.

This system led to the so-called "classical gold standard," which was put into place from the 1870s up to 1914. The classical gold standard ended with WWI's outbreak, in which gold convertibility was temporarily suspended as countries struggled to finance their expenses for the Great War.

In essence, the classical gold standard meant that any currency which was pegged to a specific weight in gold could be cashed in for physical gold. The fiat currency itself facilitated payments as there was no need for lugging around physical gold. This was a practical approach as worldwide trade picked up in the latter half of the 19th century. Thus, countries could do business in their respective currencies and settle the difference in gold.

This also meant that ships sailed all over the world with physical gold as part of their cargo.

Generally speaking, the classical gold standard necessitated countries to keep a stock of physical gold that would back the monetary mass in circulation. The purists of the Austrian School of Money posited that gold and currency should maintain a 1 to 1 ratio. For instance, one dollar would equal one ounce of gold. This system proved impractical as it was highly restrictive to expanding monetary mass.

Ultimately, countries settled on a common practice that required 40% gold backing. This meant that countries could issue two and a half times more currency than the nominal value represented in gold. So, if we pegged the one dollar-per-ounce of gold, the US government would be able to issue two and a half dollars for every ounce of gold.

Naturally, the weight of gold was measured in fractions of an ounce and could vary according to the needs of the government in question. Any time a government would move the currency's valuation against gold, they either valued or devalued their currency.

With the outbreak of WWI, governments needed to finance their war efforts. However, under the classical gold-standard rules, it was very difficult to issue currency without significantly devaluing the currency against gold. So, it proved more practical to temporarily suspend gold convertibility during the war. This allowed all of the governments involved to print as much currency as they wanted so they could finance their national wartime industries.

The best example of this was Great Britain. At the onset of WWI, Britain suspended its gold convertibility by fixing the Pound Sterling price at one point. Britain then issued as much currency as it needed to get its economy moving through the entire war. Once the war was over, Britain resumed gold convertibility but with one fatal flaw: Britain used the old gold price, set back in 1914, but without reducing its monetary mass back to 1914 levels. Considering that there was now a greater amount of currency in circulation, fixing the Pound Sterling back to pre-WWI levels caused a great deflation. The reason for the deflation was the result of Britain needing to contract the money supply to maintain 40% backing.

In the interim between WWI and the outbreak of WWII, the gold exchange standard was put into place. This system is generally considered a flawed system as it essentially pegged all of the world's fiat currencies to one fiat currency, which was, in turn, fixed to a weight of gold. This currency would then function as the world's "reserve currency".

The currency of choice for the gold exchange standard was the Pound Sterling. However, this system proved to be impractical, particularly when considering the expansion of world trade, as obtaining the Pound Sterling wasn't very practical. In fact, banks did not have the capacity to barter in the Pound Sterling. As such, various local reserve currencies popped, such as the US Dollar in America.

One interesting episode of the gold exchange standard was the hyperinflation of Weimar Germany. Since Germany had been ravaged by WWI, the German government decided to print its way back to economic prosperity. In the end, the German government printed so much money that it essentially became worthless. People were forced to move around cities and towns with wheelbarrows full of cash just to pay for groceries.

However, the old Weimar Republic's economic troubles led to the rise of Hitler and Nazi Germany. This would then usher in the era of WWII. With the onset of this new war, the world decided to suspend the gold standard once again, as countries needed to find the means to finance their war efforts. This time though, the victors, the allied nations, sought to right wrongs they had committed following WWI. One of the seasoned vets of WWI's mistakes was Winston Churchill.

At the time following WWI, Winston Churchill was named the Chancellor of the Exchequer. His office was in charge of supervising Britain's return to the gold standard. As has been pointed out previously, those efforts did not yield good results for the British economy.

The end of WWII brought about a series of political and economic changes that would then usher in a new world monetary system.

End of WWII and the Bretton Woods System

The end of WWII marked the beginning of a new era in the history of the world. Among the historic negotiations that took place, the meeting at Bretton Woods (New Hampshire, 1944) sought to bring order to the chaos that had been created following the end of WWI. While the war wasn't officially over yet, the world leaders were already preparing to set the stage for the emergence of the world following the war.

The leaders of the world's largest nations met to discuss the way the new monetary system would play out. One participant, John Maynard Keynes, was outspoken about the need to avoid the mess created by the gold exchange standard and the problems faced during the Great Depression.

This series of negotiations led to a reboot of the gold exchange standard, with the US Dollar emerging as the new world reserve currency. There were several reasons why the Dollar was the most logical choice for this reserve currency status–namely, the United States had emerged as the world's industrial powerhouse during the war. Particularly, the US's industrial capabilities had not been devastated in the same manner that Europe or Japan had been decimated.

Besides, the US boasted the world's most advanced stock and bond markets. This was an important point as it meant that the Dollar could act as a world currency due to the nature of its bond market. Additionally, the Federal Reserve System's creation in 1913 enabled the US to manage its monetary supply with greater ease than those nations whose central banks were nationalized.

Bretton Woods also brought about the creation of the International Monetary Fund or IMF. It should be noted that the IMF later developed "lender of last resort"capabilities through the creation of what is known as "Special Drawing Rights"or SDRs. In fact, the IMF's original members needed to buy in their participation by pledging a set amount of gold. This gold would be the guarantee the IMF needed to ensure liquidity in case of a crisis such as another world war.

Under the Bretton Woods system, the US Dollar's value would be pegged to a measure of gold. This is another significant reason why the US Dollar was chosen as the world's reserve currency as the US held more than 20,000 tons of gold at this time. Granted, most of that gold did not actually belong to the US, but the US was the custodian of that gold, essentially holding it in deposit for other nations.

As with the gold exchange standard, all other currencies would be pegged against the Dollar. Therefore, this was a de facto pegging against gold. However, the Bretton Woods system's main difference is that dollars could not be redeemed for gold unless a country specifically had their gold holdings deposited in the Federal Reserve. Under the previous gold exchange system, anyone holding banknotes could walk in and have his or her banknotes redeemed for gold.

This Bretton Woods system also called for the elimination of silver from circulation. Silver coins in circulation were slowly replaced by non-silver coins made of various metal alloys. The demonetization of silver was a response that most governments had as precious metals were no longer considered to be legal tender.

Additionally, exchange rates among currencies were no longer expressed in terms of gold but rather in dollars. This is an important distinction to make as the previous gold exchange standard measured all currencies as a weight of gold. This significant change is what paved the way for the petrodollar as the world's leading currency.

It should also be noted that the Bretton Woods system called for fixed interest rates. This is an important distinction as exchange rates among currencies were set by governments and not by market forces. This created an uneven playing field for a number of countries as they needed to deal with artificial exchange rates. This favored (and still does) Asian economies that could afford to export at lower prices.

Nevertheless, the greatest expansion in the history of the world took place during the second half of the 1940s, 1950s, and the first half of the 1960s. This expansion created an enormous amount of wealth as the world recovered from WWII. The past's strict international trade policies were eased, allowing export economies to do business with relative ease. The fact of the matter is that the Bretton Woods gold standard wasn't as closely enforced as its predecessor, the gold exchange standard.

Throughout this expansion, the world was flooded with the US Dollar. This positioned the US Dollar as the world's currency. However, it still played with the restriction of maintaining a reasonable gold-to-monetary-supply ratio.

Ultimately, the US was poised to become the world's leading power despite being embroiled in the Cold War with the Soviet Union. It should be noted that the Soviet bloc played under different rules. As a result, the entire communist bloc in Europe (as well as China and other Asian economies) was subject to a different set of monetary guidelines and regulations.

The End of the Bretton Woods System

Still, one of the remnants from the old standard was gold convertibility. The US had asked its allies and commercial partners to accept dollars instead of gold with the assurance that their gold was safely deposited in the US. However, the expansion of the 1950s and 60s led to a great deal of uncertainty facing the US economy in the late 1960s. As a matter of fact, European nations were beginning to get antsy about the way the Vietnam War was playing out and the looming recession over petroleum shortages throughout the world. By the early 1970s, most European nations had demanded their gold back. During this time, the US went from holding over 20,000 tons of gold to about 8,000 tons. This seeming run on the bank motivated US President Richard Nixon to suspend the gold convertibility window in August of 1971.

Now, most folks believe this was the official end of the gold standard. However, gold convertibility would continue until 1973 under special terms dictated by the US and the IMF. After 1973, the US officially ended gold convertibility. The ensuing deal the US struck with Saudi Arabia and OPEC by extension, in which oil would only be traded in Dollars around the world led to the creation of the petrodollar. This meant that the US Dollar would now be essentially backed by oil and not gold.

At this point, the world's reserve currency was essentially backed by nothing but the good faith of the US government. As long as the US was in good standing with the rest of the world, Dollars would be considered the most solid of currencies worldwide.

However, the events of the 1970s made it abundantly clear that the gold standard in itself was not the cause of the Great Depression, as some economic experts have argued over the years. In fact, the fiat currency system era has proven to be equally tumultuous as the previous standards.

One particular incident led to a loss in confidence in the US Dollar due to the ensuing recession of the late 1970s. This led the US government to issue bonds denominated in Swiss Francs in 1978 to prevent the US Dollar from falling off the map. The Dollar was saved, and despite the deep recession that dragged on into the first term of the Reagan administration, the Dollar stood tall.

With the end of gold convertibility came the end of fixed exchange rates. In the mid-1960s, Nobel Laureate Milton Friedman from the University of Chicago famously called for floating exchange rates. This was a significant paradigm shift from the Bretton Woods system. Under the concept of floating exchange rates, the market would now be free to negotiate the valuation among currencies based on market forces and not artificial, government-mandated rates.

As the world's monetary system began moving away from fixed exchange rates, wild swings became evident in various economies worldwide. This was the main reason the US passed the Exchange Rate Stabilization Act, and the European Exchange Rate Mechanism was implemented. Under these concepts, economies around the world needed to back their currencies with international foreign currency reserves, in other words, US Dollars. This implied that any country could back its currency by the amount of US Dollars held under custody.

The use of international foreign currency reserves meant that the use of US Dollars could offset any loss in confidence of a local currency. As such, any country could simply tank their own currency and do business in US Dollars, thus saving their national economy from oblivion.

The transition to this system led to the destruction of national currencies around the world. Mainly, Asian and Latin

American economies were devastated by suddenly rising exchange rates. In some countries, such as those in South America, hyperinflation took hold. This not only devastated local economies but also led to insurrections across the continent.

In the 1990s, the world seemed to have finally settled down on a new monetary system that could handle the breadth of the emerging globalization process. Now, more than ever, the world depended on a worldwide currency. The only currency that could handle the requirements was the US Dollar. The United States, the world's largest economy, was the only country that could print enough money to cover worldwide currency demands without setting off a loss of confidence.

And while the 1990s proved to show unprecedented economic growth, the early 21st century has proven to be rather complicated for the worldwide monetary system. On the whole, the world's monetary system, as it currently stands, is heavily leveraged. This is an important distinction to make because the end of the gold standard allowed the US government (in addition to other countries such as Japan) to print as much currency as they wanted by backing it with government bonds. This is something that cannot be done under the gold standard as best practices would automatically restrict the amount of currency that could be put into circulation.

Currently, there is a growing call for a return to the gold standard. However, the world's economy is far too big for a return to a fully gold-backed monetary system. The ups and downs of the past two decades have shown cracks in the US Dollar fiat-based monetary system. That is why calls for reform have been met with increased attention at international levels. Efforts such as the creation of the Euro have demonstrated that it is possible to transition to a single currency across a vast region though it should be noted that this is hardly an easy process.

The next decade will prove crucial in the consolidation of the fiat-based currency system. If wild fluctuations continue to create increased turmoil throughout the world, it might be time to revisit how the current monetary system is structured. Even with the emergence of cryptocurrencies, the world is still far away from abandoning its current monetary system. After all, at the moment, there is no other country, or currency for that matter, that could feasibly replace the US Dollar as the world's reserve currency.

6   Fundamental Analysis

An important part of fundamental analysis is understanding the role that central banks play in the economy's overall dynamic. However, it isn't always clear what a central bank is and its role in an economy. That is why this chapter is devoted to understanding a central bank's role and how it affects financial markets.

In general terms, a central bank is an institution that oversees the monetary system of a nation. This includes managing interest rates, monetary supply, currency issues, and specific macroeconomic matters such as inflation. On the whole, a central bank is circumscribed to individual countries; however, a central bank can also be expanded to manage an entire region.

The vast majority of central banks are national, meaning they are government institutions. Virtually all have independence meaning that they are not tied to any specific government branch and do not respond to the direction of a president, prime minister, or even a monarch. This independence is fundamental as being able to direct monetary policy independently means the central bank can manage its role in the economy objectively and without pressure from other sectors.

Additionally, central banks can also be privately-owned. This might seem surprising. In the case of the United States, the Federal Reserve (FED) is privately-owned by a consortium of banks. This consortium is in charge of the functions that have been outlined previously. As such, it is an independent institution and acts in the best interest of the US economy and its monetary system.

The World's Major Central Banks

The Federal Reserve Bank

On the subject of the FED, it should be highlighted that it is not a single bank. Instead, the FED is a system of banks that govern the United States' overall monetary policy. These powers were given to it in the act of Congress that led to its creation in 1913. It is important to underscore that the United States did not have a central bank before that.

In fact, the US had had two other central banks before the creation of the FED system. The first bank emerged following the revolutionary war. It was created as a means of managing the fledgling US monetary system. It existed from 1791 to 1811. The flaws in this bank's design led to reform, thus enacting the second US central bank in 1816. Technically, the US did not have a central bank from 1811 to 1816. The second US central bank functioned until Andrew Jackson became President in 1828. Jackson posited that this bank was an "engine of corruption." As such, the second US central bank closed in 1836.

This led the US economy to function without a formal central bank until the creation of its third central bank, the FED, in 1913. However, the FED's mission was somewhat different from previous iterations as it was not a government agency, but rather, a private institution. This was made by design, particularly when considering that individual banks had issued their own currency. This act is illegal but was common in the mid-to-late 19th century.

During the US Civil War, it became painfully evident that the lack of a central bank made it quite difficult to issue bonds to pay for the war effort. In fact, Abraham Lincoln's government issued Treasury Bonds to finance the war effort. It was essentially printing money without any backing whatsoever. This affected the US Dollar's value around the world. It forced the US to pledge gold to its trade partners so that they would remain at ease.

It should also be noted that up to the creation of the FED, the US's currency was issued by the Treasury. And while the Treasury still holds this right, the FED act of 1913 ceded this right to the FED. This is important to note as the current US Dollar in circulation is issued by the FED and not by the US Treasury. This is an interesting distinction as practically all countries, particularly those with a nationalized central bank, issue sovereign fiat currency under the State's name.

Consequently, the US Treasury is in charge of creating the United States' actual currency supply, while the FED is the institution that prints the actual currency itself. This is done through a process in which the US Treasury issues bonds. These bonds are put up for auction. At this auction, every major bank is invited the participate. Any of these banks can purchase the bonds though it should be pointed out that the FED purchases the vast majority of them. In return, the FED then issues "Dollars." However, these Dollars are not sovereign treasury notes. Rather, they are "Federal Reserve Notes." This is clear as these words are printed on each of the bills.

When the US Treasury seeks to increase the currency supply, more bonds are issued. In contrast, if the Treasury seeks to reduce currency supply, it simply lets bonds expire and does not roll them over or issue new ones. However, the trend throughout the history of the FED system is that the currency supply increases. In recent history, the currency supply greatly expanded thanks to the implementation of Quantitative Easing (QE) following the Great Recession of 2008-2009.

The FED is comprised of 12 banks. These banks are located in Boston, New York City, Philadelphia, Cleveland, Richmond, Atlanta, Chicago, St. Louis, Minneapolis, Kansas City, Dallas, and San Francisco. Each of these branches is in charge of overseeing its assigned region. Each bank has a chairman.

At a macro-level, the FED has a Board of Governors. These positions are appointed by the President of the United States and confirmed by Congress. The Board of Governors meets monthly to make an official statement on the direction that monetary policy will take, either by making official decisions or by issuing forward guidance. These meetings are captured in the minutes that are released to the public. The minutes are published in addition to official documentation, which may contain any, and all, forward guidance presented by the FED Board of Governors.

Like most central banks, the FED is in charge of making decisions on interest rates. Interest rates are set on the various types of financial instruments. While the market tends to set the rate at which money is lent out to individual customers by financial institutions, the leading interest is known as the Federal Funds Rate. The Fed Funds Rate is the interest rate at which inter-bank lending takes place. These are generally comprised of overnight operations and are mostly conducted to help financial institutions meet their depository reserve requirements. From this rate, the trickle-down effect on individual customers tends to be seen as far as loans, credit cards, and mortgages are concerned. The deviation is not significant and tends to move on par with the cuts or hikes the FED conducts to interest rates.

With the overall way in which the FED is able to conduct monetary policy, the FED is able to react to the various economic conditions. In general, the FED's playbook includes hiking or cutting interest rates, expanding or restricting the monetary supply (by way of the Treasury), and overseeing commercial and investment banks' operations.

The European Central Bank

With the integration of major European economies into one regional bloc and under one regional currency, the Euro, the need for a centralized European bank emerged. The need for a European Central Bank was the direct result of the founding members' acceptance of a common currency. Since the formal implementation of the European Union (EU) in 1994, the gradual phasing out of each member country's currency led to the adoption of the Euro. As such, the European Central Bank (ECB) came into force in 1998 as established by the Treaty of Amsterdam.

The creation of the ECB marked the first time that a regional central bank would guide monetary policy across a number of sovereign nations as opposed to having each nation's central bank comprise a regional body. This also created a comprehensive monetary policy that would guide each country's individual economic policy. Consequently, this forced each member State to meet specific criteria and requirements that would make them eligible for the Euro.

It should be noted that the legislation which governs the ECB is European legislation. This means that there is no jurisdiction of one single country's legal framework over the bank. Instead, the ECB is a supranational institution that is governed by treaties and agreements that all member states adhere to. Furthermore, the ECB's policy supersedes national legislation so long as it does not contradict each member state's best interest.

Under the ECB powers, the Euro acts like a currency that can be used for everyday operations by regular citizens while also enabling governments to conduct intraregional trade. As for interregional trade, Euros are generally converted into US Dollars, particularly when dealing with Asian and Latin American economies.

The ECB is mandated to expand or restrict the currency supply based on the needs of both the region and individual member states. For example, suppose an individual member state is faced with an internal crisis such as a natural disaster. In that case, it can issue sovereign bonds denominated in Euros, and the ECB can purchase them from the member state and then furnish liquidity, in Euros, for the country to spend on domestic needs.

For the ECB creation, member states were asked to pledge their own national currencies as backing for the Euro itself. While the actual paper assets were not required, the health of each nation's economy would be the backing of the ECB. In addition, 15% of the ECB's reserves were pledged in gold. Since then, the value of gold in the ECB has grown both due to the repatriation of gold by some nations such as Germany and France, but also due to the increase of the international price of gold.

Additionally, the ECB has partnerships with other major central banks, such as the FED. These agreements have opened up liquidity windows that can be tapped into during times of crisis. For instance, during the 2008 financial crisis, the Dollar supply dried up in Europe. This led the ECB to engage in a swap agreement with the FED at a 1 to 1 ratio in which the FED supplied the ECB with Dollars while the ECB provided the FED with Euros. This enabled the ECB to maintain the European banking system's overall health due to increased liquidity.

After the FED, the ECB's monetary policy has the greatest influence over the world economy. Generally speaking, both the ECB and the FED tend to be in concert at a macro-level though there is considerable divergence in each bank's specific policies.

The Bank of England

The Bank of England remains as a standalone central bank as the UK was a member state of the EU but did not form part of the Eurozone. This meant that, for political purposes, the UK was a member state[1] of the EU, but in terms of currency, the UK was not housed under the ECB's umbrella. As such, the UK continued to use the Pound Sterling as its sovereign currency, much in the same way Switzerland uses the Swiss Franc as its national currency.

The model established by the Bank of England, which was founded in 1694, is the model on which modern central banking is based. Since its 100% stake is nationally owned, it responds to the interests of the nation and not to private shareholders,

---

[1]In 2016 the UK voted for a referendum to exit from the EU (Brexit). From January 31, 2020, the UK is not anymore a member state of the EU.

as in the case of the FED or individual member states, as in the case of the ECB.

According to its legislation, it is an independent entity. This means that it can act freely without pressure from the government or the British monarch. This allows it to set monetary policy in the way that it sees fit. This monetary policy includes all of the traditional policy instruments, such as interest rates, currency supply management, banking oversight, and issuance of bonds.

Also, the Governor of the Bank of England is one of the most influential monetary policymakers in the world. The Governor of the Bank of England plays a prominent role in the IMF in much the same way the FED chairman and the ECB president do. As a result, central banking standards are closely aligned to the practices with which the Bank of England implements.

The Bank of England acts as the UK government's banker and lender of last resort to the British financial system. These are two important roles that state-owned central banks play, particularly as a part of sound fiscal management.

The Bank of Japan

The Bank of Japan (BOJ) acts as Japan's central bank. The main difference with the other three aforementioned banks lies in the fact that its ownership is mixed, meaning that it is partially owned by the State and partially publicly owned. As it currently stands, the Japanese State has a 55% stake in the bank, while 45% is publicly traded. This implies that private equity firms can own the share that is publicly traded. These are mainly private banks that have scooped up the BOJ's shares on the open market through stock exchanges.

Aside from its different ownership style, the BOJ has the same responsibilities and actions as all other central banks. So, it is mandated to govern monetary policy while also managing commercial and investment banking oversight.

Perhaps the most controversial aspect of the BOJ's policy-making has been the implementation of negative interest rates. In short, negative interest rates means that lenders, rather than collecting interest on the money they lend, actually pay money to borrowers. This seems contradictory in practical logic. But under central banking logic, this makes sense as negative rates enable financial institutions to access cheap credit, which can then be transferred to business and individual customers at rates very close to 0%.

The implementation of negative interest rates emerged in the 1990s as a result of Japan's economic crisis following a deep recession at the end of the 1980s. The BOJ resorted to slashing rates to stimulate growth. However, when the Japanese economy did not seem to rally even after slashing rates to 0%, the BOJ resorted to negative rates. Since then, the BOJ has been unable to normalize rates above 0%. This has led economic researchers to question the role of central banking in the modern economy. Nevertheless, Japan has maintained a relatively stable economy over the last two decades despite subpar growth (at least when compared to other developed nations).

Main Economic Indicators

A critical component of fundamental analysis is understanding the role that economic indicators play in the overall scope of a national economy and the world economy, for that matter. Understanding what these indicators are and their importance is a vital aspect to sound fundamental analysis.

Gross Domestic Product

The first indicator we will look at is the Gross Domestic Product (GDP). The GDP of a nation is essentially the sum of all domestic production. This indicator is vital in determining the overall health of an economy. When the GDP indicator grows, it signals expansion; thus, the economy is gaining strength.

It should be noted that there are two types of GDP calculations, nominal and real. Nominal GDP means that the GDP figures are calculated at current prices. This means that current market prices are taken into account for the total sum of domestic production. It should be noted that this figure does not reflect actual growth as nominal GDP will always show growth due to price inflation.

So, to reflect real growth, real GDP is calculated with the use of a deflator. A deflator is a statistical measure that looks to remove the effect of inflation on nominal GDP growth. This reflects the growth of GDP calculated on a base year.

GDP figures are calculated on a quarterly basis. This is important for the economic calendar as GDP figures have a considerable influence on the optimism, or lack thereof, that markets may hold with regard to the economy.

Unemployment

Unemployment is the measure of people of working age who are out of a job. As such, labor statistics generally include people over the age of fourteen in most countries though OECD countries generally include working-age people from seventeen to about sixty-five, which is the standard retirement age in such countries.

It should also be noted that unemployment rates do not

include people who are not actively looking for a job. So, even if individuals are working age, but they are not actively looking for a job, such as in the case of students, they do not count toward unemployment rates. Full employment is typically considered to be an unemployment rate between 4% and 2%. Full employment is practically impossible. That is why some leeway is taken into account when determining full employment.

Inflation

Inflation is measured by the increase in prices across a basket of goods. This is an average measure as not all products see price increases at the same time. In order to calculate inflation rates, the use of the Consumer Price Index (CPI) is needed. The CPI is a statistical measure that tracks prices over a period of time. Generally speaking, it is calculated on a month-to-month basis. Annual rates are also published by the government. Most countries' targeted inflation is set at somewhere between 2% to 4% annually. Experience has shown that this is a healthy rate that spurs growth and protects a currency's value. Ideally, inflation should be on par with GDP growth.

Trade Balance

A country's trade balance is essentially a current account of how much is exported versus how much is imported. Some countries are net importers, while others are net exporters. It should be noted that most international trade is settled in US Dollars though some countries use other regional currencies such as the Euro or perhaps the Japanese Yen. However, to ensure an apples-to-apples comparison, the US Dollar or the Euro is used as a standard currency.

Economic Calendar for Major Economies

Every country has a schedule in which they publish economic data. Generally speaking, some indicators, such as GDP, are published every quarter. So, Q1 GDP data is published in April, Q2 in July, Q3 in October, and Q4 in January.

Other data, such as CPI, unemployment rate, trade balance, payroll, industrial manufacturing, retail sector, and consumer confidence, among others, are published once a month. It should be noted that the United States publishes unemployment data on a weekly basis as unemployment benefits are collected on a weekly basis. However, most countries publish this data on a monthly basis.

For a comprehensive look at the United States' economic calendar, the site Trading Economics [2] provides the best information about the publishing date and time.

For information on the ECB and major economic indicators for the European Union, the EU's Eurostat[3] website provides comprehensive information.

For additional information on countries around the world, the IMF has a comprehensive database that provides economic data and keeps track of the worldwide aggregate data. This is a good place to start if you are looking to get up-to-date information on the world's economy as a whole.

Influence of Economic Indicators on the Forex market
When looking at economic data, it's easy to see how this type of information can influence the Forex market. While indicators do not influence the market from a practical point of view, they do influence the Forex market both psychologically and

---

[2]https://tradingeconomics.com/united-states/calendar
[3]https://ec.europa.eu/eurostat

through the valuation of a currency.

This is important to keep in mind as troubling economic data on a country, say slumping GDP figures that may indicate a recession is coming, may negatively influence investor psychology. Therefore, investors may be looking to get out of currency in favor of another. So, investors holding a depreciating currency will quickly look to move on because they fear it will continue to lose even more value in the future. By the same token, these investors may be looking to move into safe-haven currencies such as the Euro, US Dollar, Swiss Franc, or Pound Sterling in order to protect their assets. This implies that these currencies would experience a rapid expansion in their valuation, particularly compared to other currencies whose value may be declining.

A good part of solid fundamental analysis is to keep track of the trends shown in economic data. Information and analytics services generally offer historical data, usually going back as far as five years. This historical data can be used to get a snapshot of the trends in most major indicators.

In the case of the United States, the FED has a service known as FRED. This service provides historical data on several indicators. This type of data is great for producing charts and graphs, which can be used to plot trends of major indicators over long periods. In many cases, most indicators go back to the beginning of the 20th century. As such, there is data that spans more than a hundred years.

The Role of Monetary Policy in Forex trading
Monetary policy plays a critical role within the Forex market. When governments choose to expand or contract the currency supply, their currency may gain or decline in value depending

on the circumstances surrounding such decisions.

For instance, when the FED chooses to hike interest rates, the number of dollars in circulation tends to decline. This is due to the fact that both investors and the public at large would rather save their money. Investors would rather buy bonds as the yields tend to be higher. The reduction of the US Dollar in circulation causes the valuation of other currencies to decline against the Dollar as most investors outside the US would be willing to pay more for the Dollars they need. This generally drives the Dollar Index up higher.

The opposite is true when the FED lowers rates, and monetary policy such as QE is put into practice. Since the number of Dollars in circulation increases, ordinary citizens are discouraged from saving their money, while investors may be more inclined to put their money into stocks or invest in the real economy, particularly if there is access to cheap credit. This would cause the Dollar Index to fall while allowing other currencies to gain in value against the Dollar. In such cases, investors around the world are willing to pay less for the Dollars they need as there are plenty in circulation.

For investors in the Forex market, QE and lower interest rates do not necessarily mean that other currencies will increase drastically in value when compared to the US Dollar. It's important to watch the dynamic against other currency pairs, such as the Euro and the Swiss Franc, to get a general overview, as these currencies may not necessarily gain value against Dollar.

At the end of the day, monetary policy is about maintaining confidence in a given currency. When a currency is printed into oblivion, such as in the case of Zimbabwe and Venezuela, confidence is completely lost in this currency. This leads both investors and the general public to dump their currency as soon as they get it. After all, holding a currency that is quickly losing value is bad for business. Investors do not want to hold a currency that is losing value unless they can speculate on a rebound or perhaps use it to acquire real goods such as land, precious metals, commodities, or finance businesses. This is why keeping a close watch on monetary policy is an essential part of fundamental analysis.

The Role of Political Factors in Fundamental Analysis

When focusing heavily on technical analysis, political factors, which make up a sizeable chunk of fundamental analysis, tend to get overlooked. Many times, political turmoil and instability tend to get missed as a result of more emphasis being placed on numbers and trends. It is important to note that political factors can play a huge influence on the way a country's monetary policy is conducted. In addition, political pressures can lead countries to manage their economy in a less than optimal manner.

For starters, a country's openness to foreign investment is crucial in determining if investors are willing to relocate their capital to any given country. When there is a positive business climate, investors tend to feel more confident. Additionally, a strict rule of law enables investors to feel secure when opening up businesses.

On the flipside of this argument, an absence of a rule of law and openness toward foreign investment can lead to outside investment fleeing a country. This implies a considerable reduction in an economy's growth potential, not to mention the curtailing of job opportunities. In addition, not having adequate policies in place can deter local investment from emerging in the first place.

Countries that have had issues with political unrest in the past have found it hard to attract direct foreign investment once the political situation has settled down. Often, it takes years—maybe even decades—to set up a climate in which foreign investment can be attracted. Additionally, a local investment may end up being persuaded to move elsewhere as there is little confidence in what the country may be able to do to ensure investment.

Political matters also influence trade. Trade is essential for any country that is looking to expand beyond its current region. In fact, political instability can even affect trade with neighboring countries. A clear example of this can be seen in the prevalence of corruption. When a country has a high degree of corruption, smuggling can become a pervasive phenomenon leading a country to miss out on revenues stemming from tariffs and import duties.

Consequently, governments need to tackle political instability in such a way that foreign investors can view them as a "safe" country. Naturally, this is reflected in a nation's currency. As long as a political situation remains stable, a currency can be handled under proper guidelines and best practices. In turn, this leads to confidence in that particular country and its currency.

When it comes to currency, confidence plays a key role in determining its attractiveness to investors. Those investors who are not confident in a given currency may be compelled to stay away from it, as predicting its movements may become nearly impossible. Such high degrees of instability can lead to a large amount of volatility. As such, only seasoned investors who are familiar with the region should attempt to make any type of investment in a currency that does not inspire investors' overall confidence around the world.

Fundamental Analysis vs. Technical Analysis

Technical Analysis is the study of graphs. The analyst is able to understand by looking at the charts if that pair will rise or fall in the short, medium, and long term. The Fundamental Analysis instead bases its forecasts on the "fundamental factors," like news, market rumors, economic crises, political events, wars, etc.

Which is better between Technical Analysis and Fundamental Analysis? Who has never asked this question? The answer is simple: as always, in investments, there is no better, but it depends on the investor, on his way of operating in the markets, on his risk tolerance, etc. In other words, there are those who are better off with one, and there are those who are better off with the other.

I personally am more inclined to the Technical Analysis for some reasons. Let me present some of them:

- Timing: Technical Analysis offers better Timing than Fundamental Analysis. Timing is "the right time to get into a position,"the ideal time to enter the market. It is, in my opinion, one of the fundamental concepts to succeed in the Forex market. If you use the right timing, you can afford a very tight Stop Loss, so you can only lose a little.
- Flexibility: Technical Analysis is more flexible than Fundamental Analysis since it gives us key levels (for stop loss and profit target) in any time frame.
- Discount: Technical Analysis discounts the Fundamental

Analysis. This is a basic postulate of Technical Analysis. The chart already includes all the factors, all the news, all the wars, all the economic conditions, etc. As a result, if the price has risen, the fundamentals will be bullish. If the price has dropped, the fundamentals will be bearish. I can only take care of the chart, thus eliminating many variables.

In addition to this, Fundamental Analysis has the defect that certain news is difficult to find for a common investor, and sometimes when this news arrives, it is then useless because someone smarter than us has already used it and bought (or sold) before us.

We close with a sort of "metropolitan legend" of trading, a widespread belief (but wrong) that many still have today. Many investors believe that the Technical Analysis serves to make investments in the short term and that the Fundamental Analysis serves to make long-term investments. This is not true. Both can be used to operate in the short, medium, and long term.

So many investors will continue to appreciate one, and many to appreciate the other. Sometimes, using both is a good idea, thus combining the advantages of one with the advantages of the other.

Can technical and fundamental analysis co-exist?
Although technical and fundamental analysis are considered as opposite poles, many market participants have made a winning combination. For example, some fundamental analysts use technical analysis tools to identify the best times to enter the market.

Nevertheless, many technical analysts exploit economic

fundamentals to support technical signals. For example, if a technical pattern on the chart indicates the possibility of selling, we can refer to the fundamental data to obtain a confirmation of this pattern.

A mix of technical and fundamental analysis is not well received by the "extremists" of both schools of thought, but the benefit we can derive from fully understanding the technical and fundamental analyst's mindsets is undeniable.

7   Tips for Success

M ost Forex traders get into the business without having a clear understanding of the basics. If you choose to start trading before understanding how to combine the formulas or how to read the graphs, you may end up making losses. Another essential factor to consider is the Forex economic calendar. Although you may grasp the analysis tools outlined in this book, such tools on their own may not contribute to success in Forex. You need to be a person who can make personal decisions based on your analysis of the economies and of the charts.

In simple terms, you still have a long way to go as a trader, and you must give yourself time to learn the ups and downs of the market. As you learn to navigate the turbulences of this market, you should keep your eyes open and sharpen your ears. But, sharpening your ears and opening your eyes does not mean you should take instructions and advice from everybody you come across. Following the wrong source of information or not having a clear trading plan will cost you a lot of money.

In this chapter, we look at some tips and advice you should integrate into the trading strategies outlined in this book.

Focus on Reliable Sources of Information

The first and most important aspect of Forex trading that you must keep in mind is the fact that it is business. Every person who is involved in Forex is there for the money. Forex trading is a man-eat-man business. There are many people who stand out and try to market themselves as the best brokers, the best analysts, or having the best trading platform. All these entities are in for the cash and don't mind draining down your money. Every tutorial you come across or every book you meet has a catch. It is either meant to enrich the writer or to advertise for a specific broker. There are plenty of genuine materials out there that you can refer to. However, you are not supposed to give every person you come across your ears.

As a trader, you are the one responsible for protecting your interests. You must be wary of all third parties who may want to come and control your business. You are the one responsible for selecting and focusing on the most reliable sources of information out there. Some of these sources include:

Trainers and Mentors: Selecting the right trainer to follow is the first and most important step in your trading career. If you give yourself the time to select the best options for you before jumping in to start trading, you will save a lot of time in your learning process and a lot of money in your trading activity.

Before you pick a trainer in this field, ensure that you build sufficient trust between you and the person training you. This trust should be the only thing that guarantees honesty. In the same light, it is essential to choose a trainer who does not have a vested interest. If the trainer is only looking to get the cash from you, it is advisable to keep a safe distance.

If you realize that the work you are doing is not leading to any profits, you may try finding a mentor to help you step by step. The mentor can help you realize what you are doing wrong and how you can shift things around.

Financial papers: Financial papers mainly include publications that are 100% geared towards making financial analysis in the financial markets. Such papers tend to be more detailed when giving out an analysis of the market. However, when we cite such papers as some of the sources you can use, it does not mean that you should trust every financial paper you come across out there and every financial analysis they make. As a matter of fact, you should only rely on such papers for the figures and news. A financial paper gives all the data regarding the opening and closing prices of all the currency pairs. The papers give a detailed explanation of the market margins, curves, and so on.

One of the factors you need to be wary of is the constant volatile news sections. If you realize that a certain paper tends to focus on financial analysts' opinions more than the data, you need to stay away. Although analysts are allowed to give their opinions, do not be enticed into buying any currency. Any financial paper that tends to advertise a certain brokerage entity or that focuses on marketing certain pairs is flawed. You need financial papers that give you the freedom to make a choice. A good paper gives you the information in the simplest way possible. After dissecting the information, you may choose to invest in whichever direction you deem fit. Due to such inconsistencies in sources of information, you must ensure that you stick to your trading plan at all times. If you focus on your plan, no one will be able to take you away from your point of view.

Economic calendar: Another source of information is the Forex economic calendar, as outlined in Chapter 6. The economic calendar is the most reliable source of information and is one of the tools that are very vital for any trader. The first thing you should learn as soon as you open your trading account is the interpretation of the economic calendar. If you do not know how to interpret the calendar, you may miss out on some good opportunities. The economic calendar highlights some of the most important trading economic news that might have an impact on currencies. For example, for the US Dollar, the "non-farm payroll"is an essential economic indicator released every month. These economic events are organized to follow a specific course within a year. If you are trading in a certain time zone, ensure that you set your calendar to update you on all major economic activities that may lead to a shift in the currency you want to trade.

Forex Books and Academic Publications: books and academic publications are another reliable source of information. There are many books on Forex out there that can be used as a source of information. If you want to understand the subject better, you need to look for some of them. Research institutions and authors publish books and research findings each year, outlining the possibility of success in a certain financial market. Such publications are very vital and may help provide insight. With that said, these publications should only help you visualize the market.

If you want to succeed, it is reasonable to compare more than one option. Look at the available options and try comparing the different analytical results provided. If you are looking for information and trade secrets, books such as this one are vital. Different traders use different strategies. You can compare between authors and try to gather as many trading secrets as possible. With that in mind, you should not expect to make a fortune just because a trader offered his or her secret. The truth is that you have to find the trading strategies that better fit your personality and lifestyle. You have to find your own trading style that fits you like a glove. This is necessary to be able to stick to your trading plan with the right discipline. If you are looking for the most hidden secret in trading, well, this is very close to it.

Financial TV Stations: TV stations are among the most unreliable sources of financial information. One of the reasons why you must not trust TV stations is that some of the individuals influencing the news have interests in trading Forex. All TV stations are in the business of making money. The analysts they bring on their shows are also in the business of making money. The interests of the brokerage firms they represent come first before the interest of the traders. It is a matter of public knowledge that most analysts advise traders to buy assets that do not show any promising future. If you are a trader and you keep on relying on someone else's advice, you are likely to lose a lot of money.

You must realize that some of the channels you watch are also in collusion with the top brokerage firms. These firms are willing to pay to get a seat at the interview table so that they can propagate their agendas. If you are serious about making money from Forex, you have to find a better source of information and use the information wisely.

With that said, there are also some good analysts who can provide some direction for a person who is lost in the field. Knowing the right analyst and knowing what to pick from that analyst will help you stay safe in this market. Teach yourself to analyze your own data and try predicting the trends in your way.

Most amateur traders are quick to listen to Forex experts as they analyze the market on TV stations. Interestingly, many 24-hour business channels only focus on the analysis of the financial markets. These channels can break down every single detail of the market, keep viewers informed on the economic activities, and so forth. While such channels might be a good source of information, they are not a good source of analysis. In other words, if you have to watch TV, collect the data, and forget about their advice.

Some TV stations may offer information that may be helpful. For the sake of staying ahead, you should always watch the news. The general news stations inform you of all the factors happening across the world. If you are keen enough, you should be able to note major political, social, and economic activities that may affect currency pairs. This means that you should be focused on watching global news. When you watch global news, you get to know the factors that affect different economies around the world. If there is instability in a certain economy, the chances are that the currency of that country is likely to experience a drop.

Furthermore, if you only pay attention to collecting the news about the countries you trade-in, you'll make progress. For instance, if your account is in USD, make sure you know the social, political, and economic news taking place in the United States. If there is positive news for the country, expect the Dollar to gain. However, any negative news for the country may lead to a decline in the Dollar. With the news you get, try combining data from your analytical tools and use the information to grow your understanding of the markets.

The other option about TV as an information source is to watch the lesser-watched financial analysis TV stations. There are some channels that are purely focused on financial markets analysis and business. If you watch such channels, you can get some details of the Forex market. You can look at the closing prices, determine the highest gaining pairs, and the biggest losers at the end of the day. Such facts may be helpful and may inform you about global trends.

High-End Financial Websites: There are plenty of blogs that offer financial advice. If you are wise, you want to avoid any blogs that seem to only focus on making a quick buck. As a matter of fact, most blogs do not look authentic in any way. If you realize that the blog you rely upon for information is only focused on advertising the services of brokers, or it is all about enticing you to buy a certain pair, you need to take a step back. In reality, the best online sources include authentic trading websites. Several high-end websites specialize in Forex depending on the type of trading platform. If you come across a website that either specializes in MT4 or MT5, you are likely to get the right information. A good website does not focus on selling, but rather, it focuses on giving information. Some of the factors to consider when using an online analytical site include the detail of the content provided, how recent the content is, and the authenticity of the authors. You should only rely on a website that is regularly updated and one that offers verifiable information. If you are getting information from a blog, ensure that it is a blog that enjoys highly trusted individuals.

Reputable Trading Platforms: Lastly and most importantly, you can get some information from trading platforms. Most trading platforms provide a constant feed of information to help the users make informed decisions. Both MT4 and MT5 interfaces have been designed to provide a consistently updated economic calendar. Such platforms provide pop up breaking news from all regions in the world, giving the traders the relevant data that can be used in making trade decisions. Furthermore, all trading platforms offer real-time data and provide live transmission of Forex charts.

Have a Trading Plan

You cannot enjoy any success in trading without having a plan. As a matter of fact, all the details we have discussed since the first chapter lead towards creating a plan. In this case, we mean an actionable plan. Although all Forex traders have a plan, the execution of the plan should be realistic. You need a plan that can minimize your risks, increase your chances of success, and control your impulses. Furthermore, you have to create a plan that you can follow. If you want to be successful in Forex trading, you are responsible for ensuring that you stick to the plan.

A Forex plan is, in simple terms, a blueprint of everything you are going to do as a trader. The plan is a summary that has been written down in the simplest yet direct way possible. The plan must contain information on when to trade, how to trade, and what to do before and after a trade.

One crucial factor to remember about the plan is that it should be as detailed and descriptive as possible, while at the same time, it must be concise. If you have chosen to write a Forex plan for yourself, you need to be sure of the events on the plan, and you should not struggle explaining them to another person.

A standard trading plan should be about a single page or two, while a detailed one must be no longer than eight pages. Remember that you are the one who executes it, so keep it simple! Instead of writing a plan that may take a whole fifteen minutes to read, try summarizing your points so that you may find it easy to reference. When you have a simple two-page plan, you can regularly check the plan when trading to ensure that you are not making mistakes.

Most importantly, you must realize that you are the archi-tect of your trading actions. It is you who has to write the plan and implement it. This means that you need to put down actionable activities on the plan. As you learn to trade, you have to edit and update the plan regularly. Do not think that your plan is permanent and unchangeable as soon as you write it. As a matter of fact, the initial plan is just a guide that helps you learn from your mistakes. As you advance, you start correcting those mistakes one by one. If you have a good plan and keep it in your mind every time you enter a trade, you will soon realize your strengths and weaknesses.

Most people do not prepare trading plans because they think they already know all there is to know. One important factor to keep in mind when trading Forex is that Forex is a continuous learning process. Even expert traders still learn one thing or two every day. If you get into the business thinking that there is nothing you can learn, you may end up losing all your money.

Some amateur traders prefer copying a plan used by an advanced trader. While this might be okay if you are conversant with the trading techniques of the advanced trader, it is also very risky. Some of the advanced traders use techniques that are too risky and complex. If you are not at par with their level of knowledge, it is advisable to stick to your own simple plan. Instead of copying a plan, it is better to have an expert help you create an actionable trading plan for a newcomer like yourself.

Why is a Forex Trading Plan Important?

There are many reasons why a Forex trading plan is important. In simple terms, you can think of a trading plan as your guide book to trading. Forex trading is similar to gambling but not the same. It is similar because you have to stake a certain amount and predict a positive outcome to earn a larger amount if your prediction goes right. Although Forex is not a direct form of gambling, it has all the characteristics of gambling games played in casinos. As a matter of fact, one of the worst characteristics of such businesses is addiction. If you start trading without a guide that enforces discipline and control, you will likely waste all your money on impulse investments. In normal gambling games, if people lose money, they are lured into adding more money into the game so that they may recover the losses. Such stupid mistakes can make you lose a fortune in trading the markets. Therefore, you must have a plan which dictates the time you enter a trade, the time you exit, and how much capital to risk per trade.

The beauty of a trading plan is that it helps you stick to the facts. When you are using your plan, you know, for example, that you are allowed to buy at the support and sell at resistance points so that you are not pushed to buy or sell by an impulse caused by a loss. You only make decisions that are based on analytical facts and news events. As a trader, your work is to pay attention to the moving average, the oscillator, and other analytical tools that help interpret the market. If you keep trading on such tools, you will gain control of the market and make profits. This does not mean that you will never encounter losses. In the section about trading strategies, we outlined that, very often, even the most elaborate plan only guarantees, on average, just a bit more than a 50% rate of success. But what makes a trading strategy a good one is the statistical edge: if you win just 50% (or even less) of the times, but you gain on average more money when you win than when you lose, after a certain number of trades, you will end up with a profit. Thinking about this fact, it is clear you must have an enormous amount of discipline to stick to the plan when you can lose little money but a lot of times. This is the real challenge of trading, and that is why often you will hear that trading is 80% a matter of mindset.

How to Build Your Forex Trading Plan

Now that you know what a trading plan is and how important it is, we are going to create one. Although what is outlined here may not be conclusive, these are some of the basic factors that should be included within a standard trading plan. You may add other important points as you deem fit. It is also important to remember that when you write your plan, you have to describe every element so that you do not end up having items on your plan that do not have a clear meaning.

Define Your Trading Strategy: The first and most important step is to define your trading strategy. Although a trading strategy may be based on several factors, naming it gives you an easy setup of the other factors that matter. Defining a strategy entails choosing an approach that you wish to use in your trading. For instance, you may choose to use the moving average strategy, or the support and resistance strategy, or a combination of the two. In any case, you should define the parameters that determine how to enter a position and the conditions that determine when to exit a position.

Factors such as trading against the trend or sticking to the trends must be defined in this section. If you start trading without putting in place proper rules to govern your trade, you may end up making a lot of mistakes caused by impulsive buying and selling.

Define the Time Frame: This is one of the most important parameters of Forex trading that most people get wrong. Even some of the people who have been trading for a long time still make huge losses because they do not have a defined time frame. Defining your trading plan's primary time frame gives you the ability to stay focused and try to analyze the data available within that time frame. You may not necessarily choose a single time frame, but you need to have a definition of what time frame works for you and gives you the parameters to enter or exit a position. Most amateur traders start by switching between different time frames just to see which charts give more insight. Earning money and losing money depends on the way you trade and not the time frame. If you keep on switching between 5-minute charts and 4-hour charts, the chances are that you will make mistakes. A 5-minute chart has a different momentum and trend direction as compared to a 4-hour chart. It is your discipline that should help you stick to a single chart and choose to focus on the selected time frame. You can use other time frames, but not as a primary one, and only to look for a confirmation of your signals. You should choose two or three time frames that are close to each other or that are easy to analyze together. For instance, if you are interested in a relaxed trading style (not day trading), you need to choose your time frame between daily and weekly. If you are looking to position yourself on monthly or weekly trades, you can combine a monthly time frame with a weekly and a daily one. For example, you can easily calculate the moving average and compare it with the shorter time frame (multi-timeframe analysis).

The main purpose of creating a trading plan is to safeguard yourself from unhealthy behaviors. One of the common unhealthy behaviors includes constant switching between timeframes. Although you may think using multiple time frames (more than three) gives you the best chance of earning, the reality is that the more timeframes you use, the higher are your chances of losing. When you have to combine more than three time frames, you do not give each frame enough time for accurate considerations. As a matter of fact, multiple time frames will contradict every trading strategy you know.

For example, in a 5-minute time frame, you can have a buy signal, but in the daily time frame, a sell signal. This happens very often due to the macro and micro-trends in the market. With the 5-minutes time frame, it is better to keep the position open just for a few hours or at the most one day. With the daily time frame, you can keep the position open for several days. It is up to you to decide which time frame is good for you, considering the kind of trades you want and the trading style that fits your lifestyle and personality.

Define Your Watch List: The other important aspect of your Forex trading is the currency pairs that you wish to watch. In Chapter 1, we mentioned that Forex trading is much simpler and straightforward than stock trading because of the few options available. We noted that the stock market has thousands of stocks to watch, and the time needed to do all the necessary work might be limited. However, with Forex trading, you may only focus on a few pairs. As a matter of fact, there are only seven major-traded pairs that attract attention globally. If you want to succeed in Forex, you need to decide which pairs you want to monitor. It is recommended that for beginners, the focus should be on about four major pairs. If you realize that you are performing well with the four pairs, you can increase up to ten. Do not go past ten unless you are an expert. Most experts monitor up to twenty-five instruments at the same time.

If there is an abnormal market occurrence in a pair that you are not monitoring, you may be tempted to invest in it to profit from that big movement. This is often the cause of a downfall for most traders. If your plan does not take into account that currency pair, it is better you stay away from it. Investing in a pair that you have not been monitoring may lead to misinformed decisions and, consequently, losses.

Mental Preparation: Mental preparation is another important aspect of Forex trading that most traders do not like talking about. In most forums, traders are so concerned with the trading strategies and numbers that they forget the role played by the mind. You should be 100% prepared before you get into any trading business. Mental preparation entails the way you sleep and the way you feel. There are some days when you wake up feeling fatigued, tired, and sluggish. This is definitely one of the days that you want to avoid trading. If you get into trading when your mind and body feel irritated, you are likely to make trading mistakes. Neuroscientists say that the human mind tends to take the easiest way out of any situation. In other words, the brain tries to avoid thinking whenever it can. This explains the reason why you may fall asleep in a classroom where you have to learn complex mathematical equations. The mind chooses to rest rather than try to understand the equation. The same case applies to Forex trading. If your mind is tired, it is likely to let go and switch off during trading hours. You will find that during such times, a trader may resign to entering or exiting a trade position just because the signal is taking too long to show up.

Another aspect of mental preparation that you should consider is preparation for losses. One factor that you must keep in your mind is that Forex is a business like any other and that you might lose money. If you get into Forex thinking that you are going to crack it from the first minute, you may end up regretting it. Before you start trading, you must know that it is a risk you are taking and that there is a huge possibility of making serious losses. You have to be prepared to protect your money and reduce your potential losses. Furthermore, you must not focus your attention on a single loss, but on the big picture of your trading activity, and if, on a certain number of trades, your trading balance is positive. Basically, you have to start to think in probabilities.

Every morning when you wake up, and you are about to start trading, you have to assess your mind first. This should be a routine process included in your trading plan. Before you start trading, you need to have a ritual of ensuring that your mind is functional at the peak. You need to ensure that you have dealt with any doubts that may lead to low confidence. If you are overconfident in your skills, too, you need to try to reduce your energy. Having a clear and sober mind is very vital for any person who wishes to succeed in Forex and trading in general.

Your Risk: Establish your risk and reward in all the trades you do. Some people prefer to establish their risk in terms of percentage, while others only think of the risk in monetary terms. In either case, a good trading plan includes a defined risk for all the trades you take.

There are several approaches you may take when it comes to establishing your risk, as already discussed in the chapters above. Here is a simple strategy you may also use in determining your risk.

First, try determining your risk threshold in terms of percentage, say 1% to 1.5%. The best choice is to stay within the 2% limit, which is okay.

Now that you know you can only risk up to 2% per trade, you need to define your threshold. Assuming you have a $10,000 account and you are comfortable using the 2% risk as mentioned, your risk is defined as $200 on every given position. This is something that you must be very clear about to avoid making impulsive trades and end up making severe losses.

With that said, you also need to define at what dollar risk does your heart starts pounding. How much money are you willing to lose in each trade without feeling overwhelmed? For instance, in the percentage case above, your threshold is $200 per trade. However, there comes a situation where if you risk any amount above $100, your heart starts pounding.

Although $100 is only 1% of your set threshold, it is still a significant figure in your mind. It is not an amount you are freely willing to give away in a single trade. If you want to be a successful trader without having regrets about your choices, it is paramount that you define your risk threshold. You need to be very clear on how much you are willing to spend or lose on a single trade.

While it is essential to have a risk threshold that is manageable for you according to your account and strengths, you should also remember that the amount you risk determines the profits you earn.

If the trade turns out to be positive, you should be enjoying the profits based on your risk. For this reason, it is recommended that you raise your risk threshold as you gain experience. At the start of your trading, you should risk less than 1%. In this manner, you are sure you do not end up spending all your money on a business you do not understand. After several weeks of trading, you can start to increase your threshold. Once you realize that you are making significant gains in the market, you can shift your threshold to the standard 2%. Be aware that if you only risk $200, you can't expect to gain as much as a person who risks $1000. In either case, make sure that the risk is defined clearly within your trading plan.

Define Your R-Multiple and your risk-reward ratio: R-multiple (R stands for Risk) and the risk-reward ratio are basically the same things. They define how much is your potential profit in relation to your potential loss. It is important that you have a defined risk-reward ratio to help you make informed trade decisions. The trades that provide a lucrative risk-reward ratio often tend to be risky and do not come by easily. On the other hand, risks that promote a lower risk-reward ratio are more stable and reliable, plus are commonly available. When you are defining your trading strategy, you need to decide the risk-reward ratio that you are willing to accept in every trade. For instance, if you risk $50 on a position, and the potential return from the same trade is $100, your risk-reward ratio is 1:2, and the R-multiple is 2R. Another example would be where you choose to risk $50 on a position that has a potential gain of $160. To determine the R-multiple of the ratio, we simply divide the potential reward by the potential loss, in this case, 160/50, which gives us 3.2R (and a risk-reward ratio of 1:3.2).

When preparing your trading plan, you have to set the minimum risk-reward ratio. In other words, you define the minimum amount you should be earning from an investment before you choose to risk your money on it. Do not just invest in all the opportunities that present themselves. You should analyze the trade and try to determine the potential gain in relation to your potential loss. You should choose only the trades with an appropriate risk-reward ratio.

Set Entry Rules: Trading strategies discussed in Chapter 3 were meant to give you an overview of the right moments to enter and exit a trade position. When defining trading strategies, you have to consider every aspect of the analytical tools at your disposal. For instance, we had defined that the moving average should help you determine when to enter a trade based on the support and resistance points. Having a definite entry point helps eliminate losses that may be caused by impulsive intuitions. Most people often make the mistake of trying to trade based on instinct. While instinct is an important aspect of Forex trading, any beginner should base all the trades on facts. Even if you have a strong feeling that the stats are not the true reflection of the anticipated trend, you have to stick to the data.

Set Exit Rules: Entry and exit rules play more or less the same role. Entry rules help you know when to get into a trade, while the exit rules show you when to exit a trade. These rules are often assisted by orders such as the stop-loss order. Furthermore, in setting exit points, you have to consider the profits you target to make. And by looking at a chart, you can easily spot exit points with the potential profit or loss that you are likely to make considering the price setting and the possible price movement.

You must have predefined exit points in case the market goes in the direction you anticipated or in case it goes in the opposite direction. If you do not have predefined exit points, you may end up making huge losses. When preparing your trading plan, you must prioritize the process of ending all your positions in whatsoever possible scenarios. This means that your plan must have a clear definition of when to exit a trade.

The exit plans defined in our trading strategy section mainly depend on signals and stop-loss orders. In other words, the signals obtained on the chart based on your trading method can be used as an indicator to end your trade. If it turns out that the trend moves in the opposite direction to your prediction or you get an opposite signal, you should be ready to stop the trade and exit. In other cases, if you do not receive the signal, you have to exit the trade based on your stop-loss or take profit.

Risk Management: Managing risks is an essential part

of Forex trading. In every trade, there is a risk. Whether you buy or sell, you have a risk of taking a loss. The risk management strategy you use will determine your safety in the market. If you do not have a proper risk management plan, you may easily lose money.

One of the essential orders that work well in risk management is the stop-loss order. This is a key part of Forex trading that you must use if you wish to have any kind of success in the business. The stop-loss order helps you manage trades whether you are online or offline. Although this order may also limit your profits on certain occasions, it is the safety net that you can rely on to ensure that you get peace of mind when trading.

Another very used order is the trailing stop. With this, you can increase your profit while prices move in the direction you anticipated, without risking to lose it all if prices start suddenly moving in the opposite direction. Furthermore, another good strategy put in place by experienced traders is to move your stop loss at break-even as soon as the position reaches a certain amount of the profit you targeted (let's say, for example, 50% of the profit)

The ability of a trader to manage risks is what determines whether he/she will be successful or not. Most amateur traders end up quitting the business just a few days down the line due to poor risk-management strategies.

After the Trade: What you do immediately after a losing or winning trade is just as important as what you do while trading. The rules you make in your trading plan must govern you and help improve your discipline. Most traders only lose money because they use their emotions to make trade decisions after closing one. The worst-case scenario comes when you lose. Most people immediately take a new position without critical analysis, trying to recoup any losses made. This is one of the worst things you can ever do in Forex trading.

The factor to consider is the amount of time break you have to take after closing a trade. You must ensure that you take some break away from your screen and allow your mind to be interrupted by other activities before resuming your trade. If you try trading without taking a break, you may end up making the worst investment choices in the heat of the moment.

Revenge trading is when you try to make up for a loss by immediately taking a new position. The urge to make immediate compensation for the loss often leads to more losses than it leads to success. All these factors are an integral part of the mindset needed to sustain Forex trading.

On the other hand, after winning, you may also have the urge to hop on and continue winning. In the heat of the moment, you feel like you are on the top of your game. You feel like you are the master of Forex, and the urge to position again pushes you to take a bigger risk. This is another major cause of failure in Forex trading. After enjoying a streak of success, you should not fool yourself into thinking that you are the one in control. There are two reasons why people tend to invest more after enjoying a streak of success:

- They feel invincible: Once you gain success in two or three successive trades, your head is pumped up. You feel as if you are the smartest of all traders and that nothing can stop you from winning. As a trader, this is one of the mental aspects that you have to manage. If you realize that your confidence is flying above your

capacity, you need to calm yourself down and allow your
confidence to narrow down. When your confidence is too
low, you also have to motivate yourself to achieve more.

- You have money to spend: The other reason why people
  end up investing more after a streak of winning is that
  they feel like they have enough money to spend. There is
  nothing wrong with having money. As a matter of fact,
  you should know that the primary reason for trading is
  to make money. If you feel that you are in a position to
  make more money, you may be tempted just because you
  have already won. However, you must learn to control
  your impulses. If you want to succeed in Forex trading,
  get used to taking a break of around one hour after
  closing a trade. If you are trading within the one-hour
  range, you can take a break of about ten minutes just to
  allow the graph to take a different direction.

After a trade, it is a good habit to keep a journal of your
trading activity, recording the main data of the trade and the
entry and exit rules you followed. Reading back this journal as you go on with your trading will help you enormously
to understand your mistakes and to improve your trading skills.

Putting it all together: After writing down a bunch of
rules that you wish to follow for your Forex trading, you have
to put them together and write a plan. This is the hardest
part. You must remember that the plan you are making is
supposed to be used on a daily basis. If you write fragmented
content, you might have to go through a lot of work of sorting
out data before achieving your results. If you are serious about
implementing your trading plan, you have to favor all the
important points you note down. Therefore, this means that

you need to arrange your rules in a certain order.

To be able to turn your rules into a trading plan, you have to distribute them into three sections and put them into two classes. Since Forex trading happens in a process, you have to categorize your rules into the sections: before trading, during trading, and after trading.

Arrange your rules in these three sections so that you can always refer to the right section during the trading sessions. Furthermore, you have to classify your rules into two: self-discipline and trading strategies. If you have been paying attention, you may have realized that all the contents of the plan outlined above include both. For instance, the "before trading" section should have a set of rules classified as either self-discipline or trading strategy. And this is true for each section of your plan.

To be successful in trading, first ensure to follow all the trading strategies in the right way. If the strategy requires that you enter a trade when you receive a signal, the rule must be well understood from your perspective. You then need to enforce the self-discipline rules to ensure that all the strategies are put in place correctly.

8   Common Mistakes

Y ou have already learned the most important things to know about Forex trading by now. We have explored the analytical tools and the strategies that can help you make money, the main economic indicators, and how to write a trading plan. The only problem you may have for now is the common mistakes that most traders make. These mistakes are mainly correlated to their psychology. Both amateur and seasoned traders make mistakes. Some mistakes are, indeed, so attractive that even seasoned traders find themselves falling into the trap.

In this chapter, we are going to look at some of the most common mistakes that traders make that may lead to losses and how you can avoid them. If you learn to avoid these mistakes, you are guaranteed to enjoy more success than failure in your Forex trading endeavors.

The first step to avoiding all the mistakes listed in this section is preparing a trading plan, as we described in Chapter 7. Your trading plan gives you an opportunity to explore the market and make investments without improvisation and without risking too much. The plan also helps control your impulses. If you create a reliable plan and you stick to it, you should easily avoid all the mistakes mentioned in this chapter. As you plan to get into Forex trading, remember that the main cause of failure for most traders is not a lack of skills but instead a lack of discipline.

The most common cause for trading mistakes includes a desire to get rich overnight, a desire to revenge after making losses, and a hurry to recoup the money lost. All these factors are absolutely common to every trader because they are normal feelings for every human being. However, letting them prevail during your trading activity always leads to mistakes and, most of the time, to losses. For instance, traders may double losses while trying to quickly recoup their money after a loss. They apply, most of the time without being conscious, a money management technique called *"martingale"*[1]: when they make a losing trade, they double their bet in the next trade so that if they win, they will recoup their money. This technique makes sense from a mathematical point of view, but it is based on the assumption that a trader has infinite wealth to invest so that he or she can double the bet each time. The problem is that this assumption is unrealistic, and you do not know how long a negative streak will last. The most common result is that you end up losing all your money. About that, I suggest you read the story about Nick Leeson[2], a British professional trader that in 1995 caused the bankruptcy of Barings Bank, the most ancient merchant bank in London at that time. He followed the martingale technique, and because of that, he caused gigantic losses to the bank.

A better approach is, instead, the *anti-martingale* technique. This very successful technique allows you to increase your risk

---

[1]The *martingale* is a betting strategy created by gamblers in France in the 18th century

[2]*Rogue Trader* (1999) is a movie based on his story

when you are winning and decrease your risk when you are losing. So, you should do exactly the opposite of what your instinct may tell you to do.

However, the martingale and the anti-martingale are advanced techniques, not suitable for a novice trader. You have to give yourself the time to become a profitable trader first by being strict in your risk management, and then you can start to apply advanced techniques like these.

My suggestion is as long as you are a beginner trader, do not overcomplicate your life-do things suitable to your level of competence. As long as you are learning, you will introduce more and more advanced techniques in your activity.

What you should learn at the beginning of your journey if you want to succeed in Forex is the art of containment of your mind. You must train yourself and learn to dominate your feelings and act in a way that is mostly not natural, is counter-intuitive, and is extremely rational. This is, of course, not easy and needs a lot of practice to be developed. You have to train your mind and create the right mindset and attitude that will allow you to be a winner in Forex trading.

Overtrading

Overtrading simply refers to a situation where you trade for longer hours than expected, or you invest more money than you should. We have already mentioned that Forex trading can be addictive, like most gambling games. If you get into Forex without having a clear understanding, you may end up making the mistake of overtrading. When can overtrading occur most likely?

When you are making too much money: It is common

for traders to keep on investing in a trade as long as they are making money. The right time to stop trading is when you are making enough money. People who are addicted to trading do not get enough of the action. They continue trading even after reaching their profit target for the day, week, or month. For such people, profits do not mean the end of the business. They keep on investing and trying to earn more even if they have made enough profit, risking losing the money they have already made.

If you are on a winning streak, as we said before about the anti-martingale technique, it could be okay to increase your risk and continue investing. But, first of all, you must understand this technique. Then you must include it in your trading plan with written rules; you must test it, and above all, you must follow it also during losing streaks of trades. Most of the time, traders act this way not because they are following a trading plan, but because they are following their greed.

To ensure that you avoid overtrading, you need to set your trading hours. Forex is a 24-hour business. This means that you can trade at any time of the day at any place you are. To avoid the temptation to continue trading even when you are tired, set your trading hours. You should also ensure that your trading hours occur at a time when you are free. Most people who overtrade combine their trading with other activities. If you continue trading at a time when you should be busy doing another activity, you may find that the combination of multiple activities takes away your ability to trade properly due to the lack of focus.

When you are making losses: The other scenario where people get involved in overtrading is when they are making losses. Losses are very enticing. It is dangerous for a person to start making losses when there is still a lot of money in his or her trading account. For instance, if you funded your USD with $10,000 and set your investment risk at 2%, you may think that your investments are insignificant. In this case, after losing the first $200, you may think that you can recoup your money. While it is okay to try to recover lost money, you should not rely on impulse and emotions when making such critical trade decisions. Your impulse will tell you to reinvest immediately. As a matter of fact, as we discussed before, most people invest huge sums of money in the hope that they can recoup their money in the shortest time possible. The more money you lose, the more confused you get. Your mind loses control, and you eventually start making choices that are not rational.

This overtrading mistake can be avoided if you take a break. After closing a trade, whether it leads to profit or loss, you should take some time away from the screen. This is a matter of discipline. You should make up your mind to ensure that you control your actions and only make trade decisions that will impact your life positively. You must learn to accept and deal with losses since they are part of the business.

When you have too much time: The other reason why people engage in overtrading is that they have too much time on their hands. They say, "An idle mind is the devil's workshop." While Forex trading is a good and positive venture that can earn you a handsome amount of money, you should not spend your entire day thinking about the trade. As we have observed, Forex markets operate 24 hours a day. You may be fooled to think that trading around the clock is the best option for you. In reality, you should avoid trading for long hours. Even if you have plenty of time on your hands, you should try as much as possible to stick to your chosen trading hours. Engage in other activities after trading, even if it means playing games or watching movies. If you notice that you are getting addicted to your Forex trading apps, uninstall all trading apps on your mobile devices so that you may stay away from the trading platform when it is not the right time to trade.

When you lack self-discipline: The other reason why most traders get involved in overtrading is simply lack of self-discipline. If you know you are a person who lacks self-control, try avoiding Forex as much as possible. Self-discipline simply means that you have patience and emotional control. You should be able to stop yourself from taking emotional actions. The only way to survive as a Forex trader is to ensure that you follow the rules you have outlined in your trading plan. There is no way you can expect to succeed if you cannot follow the rules you have created yourself. People who lack self-control are quick to make decisions without considering the consequences. Forex trading is a game of numbers. In this trade, you must be sure that every action you take has the maximum potential of being a success. If you start making decisions that are not based on facts, you may end up losing a fortune in Forex. As you learn to trade, you eventually stop making errors that are associated with emotional instability. Your discipline will help you stop overtrading or making any other mistakes that you might have committed. To ensure that you stop overtrading, you must first answer the question of "How much trading is too much trading?"Once you know your limits, try to stop when you reach them.

Canceling the Stop Loss and Allow Losses to Run

The other big mistake that most traders make comes in the risk management section. This is a mistake that is made by both young and experienced traders. The stop-loss order is one of the most important tools that you can use to manage your risk in your trading activities. Unfortunately, the stop-loss order also limits your profits in some instances. You may feel that the price is just about to reach a resistance or support level, but the stop loss point has almost been surpassed. What most traders do is to cancel the stop-loss order and stay in, hoping that the trade may turn in their favor.

If you cancel the stop-loss order, you may result in two situations: you can make a lot of money or lose a lot of money. The fact that you can make a lot of money should never be a motivation for you to cancel the stop-loss order. Canceling the stop-loss order is a big mistake because if you follow a strategy with a statistical edge, probabilities are in favor of the stop loss, not vice versa. Any action you take in Forex should be geared towards protecting your capital and then providing an additional income. If you approach Forex with the mentality of getting rich quickly, you will likely lose all your money. There are two main reasons why people end up canceling their stop-loss orders:

A chance to make more profits: As already mentioned above, Forex trading does not guarantee 100% success even if you follow all the outlined strategies in this book. With an estimated success rate of 50%-60% based on analytical data, most traders try making a lot of money in a short time by choosing an alternative means of prediction. This means that most traders are more likely to use their instinct than follow a strategy with a statistical edge. While instinct trading can be beneficial, it is also very risky. If you keep on reading volatile news and blogs, you may fool yourself to think that you are ready for the Big Money. Those who encourage traders to make bold moves are experienced brokers. They encourage you to stop following your plan and take risks based on how you feel. Our first rule of thumb is always to ensure that emotions are not part of the business. If you spot an opportunity that you feel can lead to huge profits, avoid it as quickly as possible. What you feel does not matter when it comes to real numbers. If the charts are giving you a negative signal, it is because the odds are against your trade. Instead of trying to win against statistics, it is better to turn to more secure options. The best security option you have is the stop-loss order. With the stop-loss order, you can change the way you do your business and protect yourself from the risk of losing all your money.

Fear of Losing: The other reason why any person would cancel the stop-loss order is the fear of losing. If you are a wise trader, you understand that one position does not determine your final outcome. Trading is a probability game. What really counts is that on a large number of trades, the profits outweigh the losses. Losses are part of the game, and you have to learn to accept them. If one position turns out to be negative, you have the chance of trading on a new position and making more money. The main reason why people should protect their principal investment using the stop-loss order is that they can still engage in other trades and keep staying in business. Being in a position to continue trading even when things have gone against you is the best thing that can happen to any trader.

Not Following the Trading Plan

The other big mistake that is made by almost all traders is failing to follow the trading plan. The main reason why traders should follow the plan is that it helps avoid making mistakes. Mistakes are caused by bad choices, and bad choices cause losses. If you are in a moment of frustration, you are likely to make a mistake. However, if you stick to your trading plan, you do not give your emotions the chance to lead you to lose money. Some of the common errors that occur due to abandoning the trading plan include:

Changing your trading strategy: One of the most important factors outlined in your trading plan is the trading strategy. We have looked at multiple strategies. Each of the strategies discussed has its positives and negatives. When you create a plan, you choose whether to use one strategy or use many. The choice to use a certain strategy is determined by your understanding of the market and your trial results. Before you settle on a trading strategy, it is advisable indeed to try it out and find if it is effective according to your market analysis and if it gives you a statistical edge. Changing your chosen trading strategy midway is the worst mistake you could make. This is not only a mistake because it may lead to losses, but it leads to questioning of your full trading plan. The only reason you have a plan is so that you may follow it and utilize it to the end. If you believe in whatever you are doing, there are chances that you will make money from it. In case you choose to change the strategy, it should be because you have observed the market and analyzed it. Change your trading strategy only if you have the data to show that it is better to do so. You should have valid reasons, which can be verified by other traders.

Abandoning the chosen currency pairs: Abandoning
the trading plan means, among others, choosing different pairs
in place of the ones in your plan. In general, pairs may gain
or lose value. The fact that a pair is gaining or losing does
not mean that it is bad. Those who trade on the MT4/MT5
platform tend to be affected even more by the available options.
When you decide to trade in a certain asset, just ensure that
you stick to your asset of choice. Do not for any moment think
that because the market is changing and providing prospects
in a certain pair, you should shift to it. Those who abandon
their chosen pair often end up making losses. The fact that you
are abandoning a currency pair that you know and choosing
to follow one that you barely know immediately throws you
off balance. You cannot compete with traders who have been
investing in a certain pair in terms of knowledge for months.
You should only focus on assets you know and understand.

Trading outside the planned time frame: The time frame
of any trade is also an important part of the business. Forex
charts are displayed in different time frames, including hours,
days, weeks, and months. When deciding how to invest and
preparing the trading plan, you should select the trading period of your choice. The time frame you select helps you decide
if it is time to trade or not. Sticking to your trading plan helps
to control the urge to move from one period to another. What
happens when you choose to trade outside your chosen time
frame is that you are likely to make misinformed investments.
It takes time to study the charts and understand the trends. If
you are using a time frame, stick to it so that you do not end
up making mistakes based on a lack of analytical insight. Once
you analyze well and get the right information for a single

chart, work with it, and try to focus on making the best out of the chosen trading period.

Forgetting the rules that regulate entry and exit: The other important aspect of the trading plan is the rules that determine your entry and exit into a position. Generally, the rules are governed by your trading strategy. They are further supported by the disciplinary rules. Once you have a plan in place, you should understand that the strategy you use has limits defined by the rules you have created for yourself. Following the rules requires a lot of discipline, and many traders struggle in this field. Some traders may choose to avoid following rules after being enticed by the plan of a different trader. Volatile news and analysis may also lead some to abandon their own trading rules. If you wish to trade for long and experience lasting success, you do not have any other option but to follow the rules as outlined in your plan (if you tested them correctly). Only enter a trade when you get a signal and exit when you get the signal. For instance, if you are following the RSI strategy, look for the moments when the indicator is outside the 70-30 range and wait for it to come back into the 70-30 range before entering a trade. In other words, stick to your trading rules and let statistics be in your favor.

Focusing on Too Many Currency Pairs

The other common mistake that traders make during the early days is focusing on more than enough pairs. While having several pairs on surveillance is a good way to spot opportunities in the market, you should only focus on assets that are easily manageable. There is no need for monitoring twenty pairs when you can still trade and make an income from a single pair. Monitoring the pairs that are within your reach gives you time to get detailed information about each option. You only need around four pairs to be in a position of making money. In essence, the amount of money you make out of trading is not subject to the number of currency pairs you trade. As a matter of fact, the fewer the assets, the higher your chances of earning. Most people only make an income when they trade pairs that they have analyzed well. This entails critical observation of the pair. You can easily follow up on the economic calendar and news events that affect two countries. It is more difficult to follow up on multiple countries. If you wish to be successful, avoid the greed that may lead you to trade in very many options. For you to succeed in Forex, you only need a few pairs that you analyze well each day. It is recommended that you chose among the top seven most-traded pairs.

Listening to the Opinion of Others

The other common mistake that is made by most amateur traders is listening to the opinions of others. There are many people out there who think they are Forex experts and think that they know what they are doing. They think that they have the ability to study the market better than others. Such people may easily confuse you and take you away from your trading plan. This is the worst mistake that you could make. First, you must understand that Forex is not a black and white business. You have probably read contrasting analytical reports from two top traders. Even the most respected Forex traders in the world do not agree most of the time. In other words, everything you hear from every analyst is a matter of opinion. Instead of changing your entire plan based on an opinion, it is better to stay focused and concentrate on making your plan work.

With that said, it does not mean that to be a successful trader you have to do it on your own. As a matter of fact, it is highly recommended that you get a person who has been trading for quite some time to guide you. Such a person can help you know the ups and downs of the market. You should have a person you can refer to at any time of the day and use his or her expertise to make profits. However, such a person should only guide you and not make the decisions for you. A good Forex mentor should help you grow from one level to another by teaching you the trading techniques. He or she should show you how to create a Forex plan and how to execute it. If your mentor tries to control you, even to the extent of causing you to abandon your trading plan, you should not pay much attention. There are always people who try to show you that they know the most. It may be a big mistake if you choose to follow the opinions of such people. We have already mentioned in Chapter 7 that if someone or something tries to control your investment choices, stay away as much as possible. All the people in your trading life and the other sources of information should only be helpful when it comes to the analysis of the content. However, at no point should you base all your efforts on getting directions from a single person. Your choice should be independent and not influenced by any news outlet or third parties.

Trading for Revenge after a Loss

We have already mentioned in this chapter and in Chapter 7 the dangers that traders face when they engage in revenge trading. Revenge trading usually occurs immediately after a trader loses money on a position. Trying immediately to recoup the amount lost is one of the worst mistakes you can make. This is because revenge trading is often based on impulse and not on the trading plan. There is no trading plan that gives room for revenge trading. We have already mentioned that Forex trading requires high levels of discipline to follow your plan. If you start trading without paying attention to your personal discipline, you may end up engaging in many trading mistakes.

Conclusion

Congratulations on completing your copy of *Forex Trading*. The fact that you were willing to read all the content to the end shows your dedication and willingness to learn Forex trading. You are definitely on the right track. They say a journey of a thousand miles starts with one step; your completion in reading this book is just but the first step towards your success in Forex trading. You have now done the easy part, which is reading the content and getting it in your head. Next, you have to deal with the most challenging part, which includes implementing everything you have read.

Forex Trading is a book that makes the art of trading look practical and straightforward to all people. If you have been keen, you have observed that Forex is all about having a trading plan and stick to it. This book has outlined some of the fundamental principles that determine your success as a trader. We have looked at the vital analytical tools, such as the moving average, the oscillators, and the resistance and support points. We have looked at the relationships between these tools and some simple strategies that will help you to improve your earnings in Forex trading. We chose to focus on trading strategies that work; we have looked at them with examples, and we have provided the best and most simple content that you can use to advance your skills as a Forex trader.

Do not expect to grasp all the details in a single day. You will have to read this book over and over as you try to implement each of the concepts that have been outlined. Once you fully grasp the concepts and start implementing them, you will see everything falling into place.

Before you go, if you feel that this book has helped you to get started with Forex trading, please take a moment to post a review on Amazon. Your honest feedback would be greatly appreciated.

Good luck as you push forward to find the success you need in your Forex trading. Remember that success comes from hard work and discipline. If you stay true to your trading plan and trade with the right mindset, positive results will follow.

A Free Gift for You

To thank you for buying my book, I would like to send you a FREE BONUS BOOK, which contains the following three chapters:

1. **Main Economic Indicators in Details.** In this chapter, you will find charts with the main economic indicators for the United States, Eurozone, United Kingdom, and Japan, and a guide to interpreting them correctly. You can print it and keep it on your trading desk.

2. **Advanced Trade Management Technique** that will allow you to increase the profits from your trades.

3. **Charts and Figures.** In trading books, graphs and figures can be a problem: sometimes they are too small and difficult to read; other times, they are too much zoomed, and you lose the big picture. Thanks to this free bonus chapter, you will receive all the graphs and figures of this book, and you will overcome this problem. You will have the opportunity to look at the graphs closely and understand better what you have learned from reading this book.

What do you have to do to receive your gift?

It is very simple: go to **https://forextrading-dc86a.gr8.com**

Follow the instructions, and you will receive a PDF with the free bonus book to your email address.

If you have any question or concern, please email me at:
LarryJonesTrading@gmail.com

About the Author

Larry Jones is a professional trader and investor born in New York in 1978. He was born and raised on Long Island in a typical middle-class, New York family.

From an early age, he felt a great desire for independence and did not want to follow in his father's footsteps, who was a civil servant.

Larry discovered the world of trading at the age of fourteen when he was walking through the city and accidentally found himself on Wall Street. He was immediately fascinated by the world of the stock market, and he decided to dedicate his entire life to trading.

After high school, he enrolled in college, where he embarked on a brilliant academic career. He graduated in economics with honors and took part in a research group on the functioning of micro-economics.

During college, Larry was noticed by the most important banking institutions, and at the end of his studies, he began a prestigious career in investment banking.

After more than a decade as a professional trader and investor, Larry decided to share all his knowledge with his readers through his books–books full of practical strategies and insights that only an experienced trader can convey.